What people are saying about

In Search o

This book is filled with good idea ... s as part of a daily practice of contemplation, wellbeing, and action in the world. Drawing on a selection of inspiring early Quaker writings, Joanna Godfrey Wood translates the insights of those prophets into modern usage so we can all discover the potential of silence and stillness in our everyday lives.
Ben Pink Dandelion, Programmes Leader, Centre for Research in Quaker Studies, Woodbrooke, and Professor of Quaker Studies, University of Birmingham

In Search of Stillness is a creative and, above all, practical book of Liberal Quaker spirituality. In imaginatively adapting a simple meditation in a wide variety of ways, Joanna makes a central insight of the Liberal Quaker tradition accessible to modern-day seekers.
Mark Russ, Quaker educator, theologian and blogger

This is a beautiful resource for exploring stillness from both the perspective of early Quakers and the present time. There are many ways of coming into stillness, whether to rest, to learn, to grow and to heal. Here Joanna Godfrey Wood offers a simple meditation one can use at any time, in Meeting for Worship or in time set aside on our own. Her words draw us gently and clearly into the stillness from where they seem to flow. We see how stillness is not simply an end in itself; it is the beginning of harmony in all we do.
Ruth Tod, member of the Central Committee of Quaker Peace and Social Witness

Joanna gives us a very helpful and meaningful exploration of Quaker "stillness" along with an assortment of exercises to take us along the meditative path. She also talks about the obstacles that can block the process. I found her quote – "Explore who you really are rather than who you think you are" very helpful, and she compares legendary Quaker writings on "stillness."
Isa Louise Levy, MA, Artist and Arts Psychotherapist

Meditation, stillness, quotes, the book has all of these. A great and enlightening rendition of meditation techniques based on, and to bring out, the act of stillness. Found in Quaker meetings, this is the sense of calm as you enter the building and the aim is to find an "inner stillness." Meditation, a slowing down, a connection of mind and body: many aspects are covered, from healing to action. This book is a true insight into the nature of being "alone," being true to oneself, holding another in the Light and going within to find God.
Tony Jackson, Librarian, Muswell Hill Meeting

In her book, Joanna encourages us to explore and deepen our relationship to stillness. Her meditation, which can be adapted to all aspects of our lives, guides us towards inner stillness, which can be found at the core of our being.
Judith Wilkings, Director of Animal Interfaith Alliance, member of Quaker Concern for Animals

Being new to Quakers and to meditation, Joanna's distinction between silence and stillness was an eye-opener for me. I realise now it is stillness I seek, not necessarily silence. James Nayler's words on waiting in stillness for Light to arise out of darkness to provide guidance were very helpful and I will use Joanna's meditations to help me find the answers I seek from within.
Julia Wise, retired lecturer of law

Quaker Quicks

In Search of Stillness

Using a simple meditation to find inner peace

Other books by Joanna Godfrey Wood

Travelling in the Light
How Margaret Fell's writings can speak to Quakers today
978-0-9933627-6-7

In STEP with Quaker Testimony
Simplicity, Truth, Equality and Peace – inspired by Margaret Fell's writings
978-1-78904-577-2

Quaker Quicks

In Search of Stillness

Using a simple meditation to find inner peace

Joanna Godfrey Wood

Winchester, UK
Washington, USA

JOHN HUNT PUBLISHING

First published by Christian Alternative Books, 2021
Christian Alternative Books is an imprint of John Hunt Publishing Ltd.,
No. 3 East St., Alresford, Hampshire SO24 9EE, UK
office@jhpbooks.com
www.johnhuntpublishing.com
www.christian-alternative.com

For distributor details and how to order please visit the 'Ordering' section on our website.

Cover artwork: "Diving into Stillness," monoprint with collaged figure, acrylics, by Sally Wright

ISBN: 978 1 78904 707 3
978 1 78904 708 0 (ebook)
Library of Congress Control Number: 2020942289

A CIP catalogue record for this book is available from the British Library.

Design: Stuart Davies

UK: Printed and bound by CPI Group (UK) Ltd, Croydon, CR0 4YY
Printed in North America by CPI GPS partners

Contents

Be still and cool in thy own mind. **George Fox**

And he said, Go forth, and stand upon the mount before the Lord. And, behold, the Lord passed by, and a great and strong wind rent the mountains, and brake in pieces the rocks before the Lord; but the Lord was not in the wind: and after the wind an earthquake; but the Lord was not in the earthquake:

And after the earthquake a fire; but the Lord was not in the fire: and after the fire a still small voice. **1 Kings 19: 11-12**

Thoughts on stillness while swimming

Jingle jangle jangle
Buzz buzz ping ping
Beep cheep zoom
Roar bang bang roar
Questions questions
More questions
Some answers

Noise noise red noise
Yellow noise, blue noise
Black noise.
Information truth or lies
Or somewhere in between.
Take a breath in, deep.
Let it out
Take a deeper breath in
Then slowly, very slowly,
Push it out.

Walk away, step over
The edge, step on rounded
Stones washed smooth by
The waves.
The very cold, very clear
Water of the sea creeps up
Stinging the skin
Numbing the flesh.

Breathe slowly and deeply
Breathe slowly and deeply
Keep still and adjust
Keep still and adjust.

Still, still, float
Look up at the sky
Calm
Float within the sea
Sky above, air to breathe
Sea to support, to nurture
Caress, love, peace, stillness.
Sally Wright

Preface

About Quakers

Quakers (the Religious Society of Friends) are a religious sect grounded in Christianity, developed in England and now found worldwide. They find their roots in the English Civil War (1642–51), which raged between Cavaliers, supporters of the King, and Roundheads, supporters of Parliament. It was a time of widespread questioning and searching, and particularly religious searching. Families were divided and there was much unrest and suffering. Early Quakers, such as George Fox, Margaret Fell and others, wrote about what they had discovered in terms of spirit and worship and how what became known as "Quakerism" might work better for many people than current religious traditions. They describe clearly their exploration and discoveries of "the light" and "the stillness" and what this might mean. Their writings have been used in this book as a starting point for exploring what stillness might mean for us today and how we might use it in our lives.

The unprogrammed Quaker tradition is the style of meeting for worship followed in the UK, Europe, Australia and New Zealand and in the US (where several different forms of Quakerism are practiced). Worship involves waiting, as a group, without a minister or pastor, in silence, and perhaps in a state of stillness. There is no pre-planned ministry or order of service, though people may feel led to speak, or "minister."

Quakers usually meet for worship weekly on a Sunday, but at other times too, waiting in silence and searching within. Spirit-led action may result, including unplanned vocal ministry, perhaps sometimes involving, or supplemented by, reading from Quaker literature and the Bible. Many Friends identify as Christian, though many today do not. Both approaches are considered equally "Quaker."

About silence and stillness

Silence is a key feature of most Quaker meetings in the unprogrammed tradition. Complete silence is never realistic because people shift in their seats, wind rustles, raindrops fall and birds sing. So perhaps it is more useful to talk about "stillness," which can suggest a deeper state – an inner state that may be joined with an outer state and with a group state. Increasingly this seems to be what we are really searching for, within and without. It is clear that absence of sound, though important but usually unrealistic, is far from being the same as the experience of stillness, though perhaps silence can lead to stillness.

Stillness, inner and outer, can be searched for, and found, in religious imagery, though this is not something that Quakers generally look to. The cross may be a symbol of strength in the intersection of the two straight lines, so harsh and punishing. But at the place where this happens is a point of stillness, of nowhere-ness. It is a stopping place where nothing, or perhaps something, occurs. There may be a sense of spinning on the spot, or even drilling down to the center: of going deeper within – a ballet dancer turning on pointed toe.

Acknowledgments

Thanks to all members of Muswell Hill Meeting, North-West London Area Meeting, London, UK.

Thanks also to Ann Berne, Tony Jackson, Isa Louise Levy, Ben Pink Dandelion, Rosalind Patterson, Mark Russ, Judith Wilkings, Julia Wise and Sally Wright for contributions and feedback. Special thanks to Ruth Tod for her insights about meditation in a Quaker context and her ideas and observations, including "opening a door into a new room in meditation."

Introduction

Taking some early Quaker writings that mention stillness and silence as a starting point for exploration, and modern "translations" and interpretations, this book explores what inner stillness might be and how we can use it to enhance our lives today. It uses a basic "going within" technique referred to in this book as "the meditation," which is adapted from these writings. The meditation needs no teacher, except oneself, and it is easy to do and can be highly effective. It is useful for grounding and seeking, and hopefully finding, satisfying and healing outcomes. It can be done at any time and in any place, whenever and wherever it is needed. The meditation can be used in many guises and be adapted for many purposes, hopefully addressing some of the problems we all face in the modern world. Quaker thinking from centuries past is as current, vital and important as it ever was and it offers great richness of possibility for us today. Suggestions and examples are given as to how it might be used, but it is open to whatever adaptation might be needed.

It is hoped that this book can help readers access their own inner stillness in order to live more fully, effectively and enjoyably, starting from the experience of being in the stillness of a Quaker meeting and moving outward into the rest of life generally. It includes interpretive stories and practical exercises, poems and writings from today as well as from times gone by, highlighting discovering and healing the self before moving into action in the world. It recommends using meditative techniques in the search for stillness within Quaker meetings and elsewhere too, whether as individuals or as part of a community – or both. For example, this might involve looking at how to grow closer as a community, how to solve disputes, how to make decisions in a satisfactory way, how to discard longstanding negative feelings and learning how to value everyone equally. This means that the skills learnt can be applied to facilitating groups, in discernment and clearness processes, and carrying out formal roles. From a place of silence and stillness individuals can be helped to focus on the issue at hand and seek guidance as a group rather than seeing things from an individual position, arguing and getting into confrontational, entrenched positions. Forgiveness can come far more easily. We explore how a period of stillness in a group can make all the difference to outcomes.

Today

Life can be full of stress – or at least it sometimes feels that way. It is our natural response to pressure. Long-hours' work, life-balance issues, relationship problems, financial worries, job insecurity, exposure to fake news and technological threats, health problems, political issues, too many commitments and too much to pack into the day – all these things work against finding a sense of enjoyment, peace and fulfillment in life. Many find the material side of life shallow – it sometimes feels as though we have been sold a hollow dream. Religion might come to our assistance, but it is frequently found unsatisfying. Proscribed beliefs seem far from credible in this scientific age. The model of "God out there," as still expressed in many religions, and remaining a common mindset, perhaps taken too literally, no longer works for many, even though they might acknowledge a power beyond the self. Instead they "throw the baby out with the bathwater," saying, "Well, I can't believe in that, so none of it is for me." The idea of finding a unique, personal path while remaining at home, secure in an established religion may not seem right if someone is used to "receiving" wisdom from others who seem more learned or qualified. The concept of a "higher power" may grate on many ears and hearts these days, but if pushed, some will know the presence of "other" and have experienced "otherness" in life, whether in the form of unbidden moments of deep insight or longer spells of enhanced meaningfulness, when all of existence seems to be charged with awe, mystery and wonder. Each person can interpret such things in their own way, according to their own Light. From this position, there is a better chance of finding a place, meaning and purpose here, part of life on earth and we may feel better able to deal with its challenges and reverses. The positive aspects of life gradually seem to dominate over the more negative ones and this soon becomes a regular phenomenon rather than occasional – more the norm of life than a rarity.

Within Quakerism there is much spiritual seeking, possibly more than in former times, except perhaps at the time of the English Civil War in the seventeenth century. Many different searchings and findings live together under the Quaker umbrella, though we are mostly agreed that there is no certainty that we will ever discover anything, but perhaps there are "findings." Stillness has a big part to play in this: while we are searching we can wait in stillness. In fact, there is little else we *can* do. A place of stillness may help us to find more, while we may find a place of stillness via a simple series of prompts or steps, taking us on a journey of continuous surfacing and diving down again. Moments of insight or deep understanding may be only fleeting, but they shine more brightly, like stars in a black sky, because of that. They are all the more memorable because they are so hard to hold on to.

Part I

Origins and Beginnings

Poem in lockdown

On this summer's evening
the gentleness of alone-ness
the stillness of silence.
Only the magpie hops across the lawn at a great pace
Where the children had blown ephemeral bubbles.
Grandma played with grandchild
Young boys kicked footballs
that I tried to retrieve from under my bench, always out of reach.
The beauty of the walled border flowers, wild yet tamed by artistry
This lawn where I entertained with jazz song
Where thespians ran riot à la Shakespeare
The lawn where mother, father, friends, lovers, relations lie lost to life
All are with me now in this sweet twilight evening.

Isa Louise Levy

Chapter 1

The Meditation

This book is about rediscovering a quick and easy technique for going within to find inner stillness, borrowing some founding Quaker principles and ideas originally presented by early Quaker George Fox and others. The meditation can be used in many different ways and can be adapted in whatever way you need, for whatever purpose: whether to calm, center, find focus and direction, enhance existing skills or explore new ones, or help solve problems. You can find confidence in using your creativity, problem-solving abilities to access Spirit, find wholeness, be of service, find "otherness."

The meditation is really just an ordinary meditation, but using words as steps to go deeper within. Mantras and other prompts are offered too. If the steps seem too complex, or perhaps forced, try adopting "Still" or "Stillness" as your personal mantra.

It is hard to describe what meditation is and what it can mean in daily life. Perhaps it is better just to do it and then feel the difference in yourself, accepting it for what it is as practice continues and time goes by. If you observe benefits, then it is worth the time you have put in, even though results, as such, may not yet be obvious. Meditation is a real slowing down and connecting up of the mind and the body – finding your whole integrated system: it brings everything into one thing – You.

So, it is good to find mindfulness in the mundane, in putting one step in front of the other, even perhaps finding enjoyment, or at least finding that the most irritating things are not so irritating after all. You do not need to rush and every moment matters. It can mean the difference between finding the positives and not finding them, seeing the light rather than the darkness, finding meaning rather than hollowness.

You may find that words are not enough for you: feeling and visualizing needs to be there too for everything to make sense in the round and to feel effective. You will find that many of the meditation examples provide suggestions for ways to form helpful mental images in practicing meditation. In that way, you may be able to explore the full weight of an idea rather than just thinking about it as an abstract.

What is stillness?

Inner stillness lies at the core of our being, deep within. It is the space, or the void, where the soul might reside. It is where the world stops turning and where we can find rest. Experiencing this sense of stillness can give life meaning and propel us forward into action, for the good of ourselves and of others. It can give us a strong sense of knowing what is the right thing to do next and the feeling that we can do it with confidence, from a place of personal strength and awareness of the still center.

But how can you find this stillness? It comes unbidden in flashes of awareness, though simply knowing about it and thinking about it is helpful. You start from a place of silence, which may not necessarily mean complete quiet, which is impossible, and move to a different place, where there is nothing. You can achieve this by pausing activity and going within just for a moment. Or you might find the same place while doing other things. Some activities lead naturally to you finding stillness, for example, being in a Quaker meeting, practicing yoga, meditating, and many activities when performed mindfully.

Stillness does not necessarily arrive because of the presence of silence – it can be experienced unexpectedly in a hubbub of noise, action and a general mood of discomfort or awkwardness. So it may come unexpectedly in the midst of life and it does not rely on you making space for it to arrive.

* * *

An example of unexpected stillness:
In the frenzy of a fish market, people rush back and forth, shouting and laughing, talking. There is color, vibrancy, aromas and tastes, traffic exhaust fumes. There is flamboyant cooking, smoke billowing, enthusiastic eating, shouting, music. There are people break-dancing on rough concrete and there are small children gyrating on an open stage. There is dusty earth and discarded paper. There is something thick and sticky dried onto the tabletop. There are flimsy white plastic chairs and single-use knives and forks. There is the most delicious plate of food you have ever tasted. A man dressed only in a pair of harlequin trousers and flip-up sunglasses holds a small monkey in the crook of his arm. The monkey has pierced ears and wears a heavy gold necklace. There is a drunk, swearing man and girls laughing nervously, dressed in revealing hot-weather clothes. We have strayed far beyond the borders of our usual lives, but there is peace in this place and there is peace within. There are many things here to feel at odds with, but at the center there is a sort of calm, a still place, and a kind of belonging.

* * *

An example of waiting for stillness, which did not appear:
The colorful cushion sits invitingly on the soft, tempting carpet in the quiet sunny room. The incense hangs seductively in the air. The atmosphere seems perfect for a meditation session: temperature just right, calming background sounds, mood tranquil, body relaxed, thoughts not invading, worries at rest. Everything is set up for the meditative state to find a home. Time passes and the clock ticks. Breathe in and out. In and out. Over and over. More time passes. In and out. The mind wanders and comes back to the breath again. The same happens. And again. Random thoughts spring into action. Come back to the breath again. And again. Annoyance creeps in. Try and

try again; too much trying. Too much forcing. Guilt about not trying. Give up and go and do something else? Try again tomorrow. It seems as though nothing has happened. Or has it?

* * *

How this book came about

If someone is told that they have a serious disease, in that moment of revelation and realization the world stops. As the information is absorbed, the person gradually becomes aware of the fact that they might not live much longer, that their life might be curtailed at the very time when it feels as if they might be just getting started. The awareness sinks in that they might never get to do all the things they have been waiting to do, or wanting to do, or waiting to be ready to do. So this book comes directly from a moment like that, which was indeed a moment of stillness, though unwanted. Perhaps, when we receive challenging news like this, we resolve to start doing things that really matter in the time that might, or might not, be left to us. Moments of realization teach great lessons: we must do things while we can. We must not leave things until "later"; we must use time well, while we still have it. However, the idea that disease might return one day keeps us alert. Writing this book was an experience of exploration and discovery, not to mention great healing. Things to write about emerged just as they were being put down on the page – one idea led to another. The "doing" of it helped and was part of the search for stillness and the finding of it. The book was written from a place of stillness.

* * *

Sometimes your mood and what is in front of you coincide to create a moment of stillness. When this happens, you will experience a mundane event taking on great significance. But you may not yet know why. An inscription on a plaque in a church had this effect. The building was perched on a clifftop overlooking the sea. The graveyard afforded the dead in their tombs a magnificent view. The poetic rhythm of the words and their flow, just like the waves, caught me and held me in a moment of stillness. I was also affected by the poignant and piercing expression of grief for a loved one:

This monument
is inscribed
by conjugal affection
to the memory of
a beloved wife
Sarah Ann Haynes
who
in the bloom of youth
and of health
was in a moment summoned
by the wisdom of providence
from the cares of this world
to
the hopes and expectations
of a better
died July 30 1824
aged 27 years
three helpless infants
pledges of mutual affection
the objects of her
tenderest anxiety
and most watchful care
alike deplore her
untimely fate

* * *

Perhaps we all crave silence and it is a default setting, if it can be found, though this may be almost never. If this is the case, we must push further, for stillness. Silence is hard to find, but perhaps stillness is more accessible. To be in a state of stillness is to get some way towards being in the center of what *is*. It is to become aware of something and to be in the flow of life. So when we are asked, perhaps, to "wait in stillness" in Quaker business meetings, it is far more than a request to stop talking and moving about. We are asked to dive within, to an epicenter of the self, to a place of inner awareness, where we might find common ground and be joined as one; where Truth resides and knowing might be found.

Stillness is the key to carrying out almost any skill or performance successfully, unless it is a reflexive fight-or-flight action to get away from danger. Pause for a moment before you act, to go within. A brief moment of composure will help you face many difficult situations and carry them forward to a positive conclusion. If you feel anger or fear welling up, try accessing stillness very briefly before reacting – or at least remember its existence. It might stop you lashing out and making things worse – acting in a way you later regret.

I was standing at a busy crossroads waiting for lights to change. Traffic was racing by, people buzzing back and forth; noise and fumes, action, restlessness, rush, impatience, thoughts, demands. Suddenly and unexpectedly, I felt my whole existence pause. I looked to see whether the green man was showing yet, followed by the pressurizing countdown of seconds allowed to cross the junction, people crossing over each other. But I felt strangely calm and quiet. I felt "otherness" deep within, a stillness, and my whole life shifted into the present. My mood lifted and I felt focused, renewed and in the right space at the right time. I realized that I didn't need to be sitting in a calm space, either at home or at a Quaker meeting, to experience stillness. In the noisy outside world, it was alive, and there, always, as a tool to be used whenever I needed it.

Stillness in creativity; creativity in stillness

The more we can find stillness, the more creative we can be – and the more creative we are the more we can find stillness. Creativity is a key tool for finding stillness. Repetitive activities can act to calm and still us in an almost magical way. It seems as though the hands' actions send messages to the brain to detach and instruct it to become more still. This soon becomes a reflexive response and for many people the "doing" of the work, the repetitive, totally satisfying, actions are where we can find deep stillness within, so that the passing of time recedes into the background, ordinary life is put aside and we become at one with what we are doing. The finished work means so much because of the stillness that went into the doing or making and the creativity that was released as a result.

However, creativity in making and doing is not for everyone. If producing art or writing is not something we do ourselves, then we can appreciate other people's and share the process that way. Some styles of writing are more calming than others and speak to our souls in a way that others cannot. This is why some people return again and again to a much-loved writer or a book that they find relaxing because it removes them from the world briefly and allows them to find their stillness again. This can be particularly true of books that were written long ago because they describe slower times and may seem soothing, reassuring. Sometimes the writer has taken more words to say something than might be the case in a modern book and this has the effect of slowing the reader right down.

Looking at art can have the same quieting effect. Drinking in the energy of a real painting or artwork while standing before it is an activity in and of itself; really looking at details and fragments, brushstrokes and the way the piece is working, the intersections of light and dark, juxtapositions of colors, tones and textures. Deserving more than a quick glance, the piece can be observed from a place of stillness; we can recall and revisualize it later. A real painting has the quality of being "alive." It is like the difference between live and recorded music. Gazing at an artwork, with a soft focus, from stillness, sets the mind free and thoughts can float. Maybe there is more there than you initially thought. Perhaps there is something there that even the artist was unaware of, or you are suddenly struck by an unexpected insight, which arrives quite unbidden; a new meaning hits you and the work now has an added resonance not noticed before. Maybe there are layers of significance that peel away to reveal previously hidden depths of color and texture. Perhaps the presenting subject of the painting is only on the surface and there is more there that is not immediately obvious, deeper down, within. Or thoughts come up about the artist and the circumstances in which the piece was created. It may help to avoid supporting information because this might steer thoughts in a specific direction. Focus on the dynamic between you and the art and work with that, looking at your own feelings and responses to what is before you. Any activity like this can produce long-lasting stillness to carry us through life, rather than just fleeting moments that vanish quickly, which cannot be recaptured, to exist only as shadows in the memory.

Stillness in Quaker meetings

A good place to start trying to find, develop or increase, the stillness in life is to go to a Quaker meeting. This is a place, which seems fairly unique, where you can search freely for stillness within and find it individually and in community too, as a connected group. You will feel part of the group even if you do not know the people individually yet. It is the stillness that binds you and creates the group. There is great peace available for all. It is there, reliably, every week and the awareness of this can sustain one through a week of stress and difficulty. It can restore one to oneself and put everything back into perspective. Sitting with others makes it different – a group activity. There is also much there available for the individual. Quaker practice, including the meditation described in this book, helps you to see how to build a structure of Spirit into your life, if that is what you want and need. It is also a good way to take a close look at issues that are individual concerns, in a supportive, non-judgmental way, open to, and held in, the Light. In short, Quaker meditation can help us to help ourselves.

When you enter the building, cross the threshold, you will sense a still atmosphere. You enter a different kind of space and way of being in the world. The collected stillness of many Quaker meetings over many years, decades and centuries seems to be part of the fabric of the building and is almost palpable, but similar atmosphere can be felt in online meetings for worship too. You instantly feel calmer and the expectation of calmness every time you attend meeting becomes more and more predictable and certain over time. The plainness of meetinghouses allows no visual distraction and lends a feeling of honesty and truth to the surroundings. Unadorned, the meeting room presents itself to you: come in, sit anywhere, relax, leave your everyday life at the door for a while. Perhaps you give a sigh of relief to be there. As you sit in the silence, gradually people come in and join in with it. It becomes a group silence and perhaps a group stillness. All are together in it.

Getting started with a basic meditation

When you meditate on your aim to find stillness in life, it will come to you unbidden. It is there whenever your thoughts flow towards it. Wherever you are. It is within. You just have to put yourself in the right place and space.

To get started with meditation in general, before moving on to the meditation featured in this book, try the following introductory version. If you don't want to use the breath as your centering tool, choose a meaningful word as a personal mantra. Whatever works best for you is the important thing. Start off by spending just a few minutes and gradually extend the time as you get used to it. Try to do your meditating at the same time every day, and if possible in the same place.

- Sit or lie down comfortably.
- Relax, close your eyes or adopt a soft gaze.
- Breathe in and out normally.
- Turn your attention to your breath as it passes through your nostrils.
- Notice the coolness of the air.
- When your thoughts stray, turn them gently back to the breath.

Afterwards, observe how you now feel. Perhaps you are generally more relaxed and able to take on the world. Perhaps things seem to have fallen into perspective a bit better than before. Perhaps you feel calmer and anxious thoughts have melted away. It will be different for everyone. Answers to questions, if you receive them, may arrive straight away. But they may not. Or they may not be clear-cut "solutions" to a problem. Or they may come to you later, when you are doing something quite different and your mind is released. You may need to repeat the meditation a few times and perhaps note feelings and thoughts to ponder another time. The meditation can be like opening a door into a new room and you may need to look inside first before you can absorb and appreciate what you are looking at. You may need to spend time in this room and assess it properly, before you understand what it is you are seeking – and finding.

Chapter 2

Looking at Some Early Quaker Writings

Thought turning into healing

Once there was a thought
And it was a good thought
It was the right thought

Once there was a feeling
And it was a good feeling
It was the right feeling

Once there was a word
And it was a good word
It was the right word

Once there was an action
And it was a good action
It was the right action

Once there was a healing
And it was a good healing
It was the right healing

There was no better way of thinking, feeling, speaking, acting and healing.

JGW

This section explores brief passages from the writings of some Quakers of former times and what they said about stillness. It gives some biographical information followed by an "imagining," in an attempt to bring the character to life in a small way. All the readings (in alphabetical order), with the exception of Margaret Fell's, are to be found in *Quaker Faith and Practice,* 1994. Before that, we start with a short quotation from Chapter 3, General Counsel on Church Affairs:

In our meetings for worship we seek through the ***stillness*** *to know God's will for ourselves and for the gathered group.*
Quaker Faith and Practice, 3.02

Advices and Queries are guidelines about how Quakers might live out faith. Embodied in the 42 pieces of text are varied issues applying to our lives and living in faith. Advice number 8, below, explains what worship is and what stillness might have to contribute to that state. The advice leads rather than instructs, hinting at the "how" rather than the "what" or the "why."

Worship is our response to an awareness of God. We can worship alone, but when we join with others in expectant waiting we may discover a deeper sense of God's presence. We seek a gathered ***stillness*** *in our meetings for worship so that all may feel the power of God's love drawing us together and leading us.*
Advice number 8

Rather than constantly feeling we, as modern Quakers, have to keep reinventing the wheel and thinking that we have to explore Quakerism from where we are "now," in our lives today, before moving forward, it might be good to look back to the very beginning of Quakerism in the seventeenth century. Perhaps we can see what their first principles were and why Quaker practice stood out as so different and so important for these seekers. They are telling us to look within rather than outside ourselves; a key difference between early Quakerism and much of the religious practice of the day – one that works well for us today.

Margaret Fell, 1614–1702

Fell was one of the first Quakers. She went through a convincement experience when she first met George Fox, then an itinerant "seeker," whom she eventually married in 1669. Together with others they masterminded what became the Quaker "way." Fell made an important contribution, providing not just an administrative hub in her home and with her family, welcoming traveling seekers and preachers and giving them hospitality, but also providing an important focal point from which the Quaker movement could be organized and launched into the world. A person of great strength of character, imprisoned for long periods in conditions of hardship and cruelty, Fell's spiritual experiences and writings concerning the "Light" and her forthright words of encouragement continue to be a key inspiration for Friends. It seems clear that Fell's initial search for another way of relating to God is very much part of her eventually finding it. She is receptive. So that when she encounters Fox, she is ready to embrace what he has to say, finding the Truth within and then going on to explore it further and build on it for herself and for others.

An imagining

A mental image of Margaret reveals a tall, slim woman wearing a bonnet and shawl, long woolen skirt, striding down a country path, the owner of the land she is walking on and the manager of the farmland that surrounds her. She is mistress of all she can see. She is taking the air on a warm spring morning, confident in the knowledge that her farm, her house, her children and her land are well tended in her absence. Her husband, Judge Fell, is away on the circuit. She is strong and independent and she runs her own life. She has stillness at her center. Today, she is enjoying a moment's peace to sustain her before she goes back to attending to the estate accounts and a sick servant, plus a multitude of other important responsibilities. She cares for her household with kindness and firmness, with great assurance, and they love and respect her in return. Her boots are sturdy. The sun is out. The birds sing. The day will progress calmly, in the way that she has planned for it.

From her writings
My Dear Hearts, God is Light, and in him is no Darkness at all, the work that he works, is in the Light, which is pure, and leads to purity; which Light testifies against all Sin, and all the deeds of Darkness, and all Earthliness, Lust, Pride, and Covetousness, which is Idolatry, whose Minds turns from the Light, turns into the Idolatry, and into the Sorcery, under the dark Power, and into the Witchery, where the Devil hath Power.

Therefore if you love your Souls, which is Immortal, abide in the Light, and Love the Light, and walk in the Light, where the Fellowship and the Unity is – For if you walk in the Light, and abide in the Light, which is Low and Meek, and wait in ***Silence*** *and Earthliness, and Obedience, wait Patiently, and you shall have the Light of Life.*
Margaret Fell, *A Brief Collection of Remarkable Passages...* (p. 48)

Adaptation
Dear Hearts, God is Light, and there is no darkness to be found in it. The work of that of God is in Light, which is pure in itself and also leads to more purity. The Light works against negative things, dark things and the base things of life and all things that turn away from Light, into darkness, where evil has power.

So if you love your innermost soul, stay in Light and love it, walk in it, where there is fellowship and unity. If you walk in Light and stay in it, quietly and patiently, you will find that you have the Light of life.

Further thoughts
Fell draws us into the Light, and asks us to wait in silence (or stillness) for the Light of Life to come to us. There we will find the strength to struggle against the "darkness" of life.

From her writings
So when you meet together, wait in ***silence*** *upon the Lord, that you may come to know the invisible Vertue and Life which comes from the living God, that ye may know what it is to eat of the hidden Manna. And so the Lord God of Power keep you single in your Measures, up to himself, that in the Spirit ye may wait, to worship him in Spirit, who is a Spirit. And this was I moved of the Lord to write to you in Tenderness and Bowels of Love to the Seed of God, for which my Soul travels, that I may see it gathered into the Everlasting Covenant of Love, Life and Peace, by the Word of Reconciliation.*
Margaret Fell, *A Brief Collection of Remarkable Passages*... (p. 505)

Adaptation
When you meet, wait in silence on that of God, so that you can know the very nature of it, and what it is to benefit from Spirit. That of God sees your potential, so that you can do your best according to it. I was moved by that of God to write these thoughts from my heart in that of God.

Further thoughts
These passages from Margaret Fell's writings exhort us to seek silence and work from a place of silence, so that we can fulfill our various different potentials and operate our truth in Spirit.

* * *

George Fox, 1624–91

Fox is perhaps the most well known early Friend and one of

the main founders of Quakerism. What seems to be relevant to this book, which places meditation and mindfulness at its heart, is how Fox seemed to be living very much in the moment, at least at the beginning of his career. He exists experientially and everything that happens to him does so as a result of his search for Truth. He is open to Truth within and that leads him to it. He left home as a young man without a plan and was "seeking" in an open-ended way. He seems to have walked out spontaneously, seeing what the day might bring, prepared for anything and he made many great discoveries in the course of this: visions, healings and the "convincement" ("conversion") of many he came across.

An imagining

George walks with only a vague idea of where he is going. In some places people welcome him, but in others they are hostile. He never knows where he will get his next meal or be able to lay his head that night. He is beginning to put together a mental map of where the friendly, welcoming people are, where he can count on warmth and hospitality. He has become relaxed about what might or might not happen, today, tomorrow or the next day. It is fruitless to worry. There is only the "now." He is on a mission, which has taken over his entire life. This is to tell anyone who will listen about discoveries he has made concerning Light, but he never knows whether people will listen, with faces upturned in rapture, or whether instead they will seize the nearest jagged rock to throw at him. The way is hard and though his boots are solid, he has only the cloak on his back and his leather trousers to protect him from weather – and other things. Sometimes he feels quite unhinged, but at other times in possession of the answer to everything. Sometimes he is unsafe and fearful; at other times perfectly secure and at peace with the world.

From his writings

Be ***still*** *and cool in thy own mind and spirit from thy own thoughts, and then thou wilt feel the principle of God to turn thy mind to the Lord God, whereby thou wilt receive his strength and power from whence life comes, to allay all tempests, against blusterings and storms. That is it which moulds up into patience, into innocency, into soberness, into* ***stillness****, into stayedness, into quietness, up to God, with his power.*

George Fox, 1658 (*Quaker Faith and Practice*, 2.18)

Adaptation

Be still and relaxed in mind and spirit. Let your thoughts go. Then you will feel the way of that of God to turn your mind to it, in which you will receive the strength of life, to calm your jangled thoughts and worries. This power is yours to use patiently, adding to the stillness already within you, returning it to the power of life itself, for the good of all.

Further thoughts

Reading over some of Fox's writings, in his *Journal*, is salutary. His daily life was difficult. He was an itinerant preacher initially and encountered much hostility in those he came across in his travels, and in those who heard him preach. He was beaten and shouted at, suffering many vicious attacks, turned away when he was cold, hungry and tired. And when he was imprisoned he was treated little better than an animal. The violence and deprivation, lack of humanity was extreme but Fox nonetheless felt love for those who persecuted, even as they carried out their wicked acts. This background of great pain and cruelty makes the "stillness" mentioned in his writings even more moving. How could he have had the strength and patience to make such sublime discoveries during such extreme hardship? The advice we read of in this paragraph is like a step-by-step guide to stillness: instructions. We are to: be still, turn to God, receive strength. It seems so simple and so immediate: that is all we have to do.

* * *

James Nayler, 1618–60

Nayler was a well-known early Quaker. Like Fox, and perhaps prompted by him, he makes the decision to leave everything behind in order to "seek." He has a vivid sense of the living Christ within him, which comes after much prayer, deep thought, seeking and revelation in stillness. He has a hard time convincing others, and possibly himself, that his calling really does come from God rather than from his own ego. He, probably unwittingly, attracts adoring followers, who want him to declare himself as the Quaker leader, possibly confusing the living Christ within with the historical Jesus. This perhaps gives others the wrong idea – that he believes himself to be above others, even Christ – whereas he only wants to demonstrate that he has "Christ-ness" within him. His Truth eventually manifests itself in terms of "going as a sign" (when a person felt the spirit so strongly that they were compelled to act out their experience in public; an outward manifestation of the inner state), and this is much misinterpreted.

An imagining

James works on his land, but it dawns on him that he must leave this life, at least for a while. Without even saying goodbye or packing a bag he sets off, with only a vague idea of where he is going or what he will do. He feels inward compulsion, a "calling," which he wrestles with and which makes him ill. Eventually this calling will lead to him experiencing the spirit of Christ so strongly that he climbs onto a donkey and rides Christ-like into Bristol. He does not even understand quite how this comes about. Perhaps he is carried away by this revelatory act and has succumbed to something dangerous – being revered and put on a pedestal by adoring followers. Perhaps he has misunderstood his own calling. His demonstration of deeply experienced faith causes great offence, and he is tried for blasphemy. What did he understand about God and himself and what were others seeing in him and in his actions? However, today, he feels troubled that he has not given time to his family before leaving home or made the proper preparations. Did he even say goodbye? He cannot remember. But he knows that Anne will forgive him in the end – and she does. The Light within is his guide and wherever it leads, prompts and nudges, James follows, without question, for the Light has full authority. The stillness within leads him to the Light.

From his writings
Art thou in the Darkness? Mind it not, for if thou dost it will fill thee more, but stand ***still*** *and act not, and wait in patience till Light arises out of Darkness to lead thee.*
James Nayler (*Quaker Faith and Practice* 21.65)

Adaptation
If you feel depressed and in a state of darkness, don't worry about it or take too much notice of it because it will make things worse and the sense of darkness will take a greater hold of you. Instead, stand in the stillness that is deep inside you and wait patiently for Light to come out of that darkness and tell you which way to go next.

Further thoughts
Standing still, without doing anything and waiting may feel reassuring in our tendency to be busy and to be constantly doing something. However, sometimes "doing" does not serve us and we need to pause, be still and let Light come to us instead. Nayler's words are inspiring to those of us who may feel that

we need to control everything in life, that we are responsible for all. Sometimes it may be better not to act but to let go instead.

* * *

Alexander Parker, 1628–89

Parker, a Quaker writer and traveling preacher, was one of those who set up Six Weeks Meeting in 1671.

An imagining

Alexander preaches and writes, traveling in ministry, and he has a strong sense of order. He knows what needs to be done and he gets on with it. His faith has logic and simplicity. He follows the practice that he has found to be effective and he acts from a place of confidence in it. If he could spread the word, he knows that others would find the same qualities in it.

From his writings

Sit down and turn in to the same light, and wait in the spirit; and so all the rest coming in, in the fear of the Lord, sit down in pure ***stillness*** *and silence of all flesh, and wait in the light.*

Alexander Parker, 1660 (*Quaker Faith and Practice* 2.41)

Adaptation

Sit and turn inward to access the same Light and wait there in spirit; as others come in too, mindful of the presence of that of God, sit and in gathered stillness and silence, wait in the Light.

Further thoughts

Parker seems to be a no-nonsense, practical person: scholarly, thoughtful and experienced. His words are reassuring and inspiring in their simplicity. He gives sensible, step-by-step instructions that read like a self-help book: "Do this, and you will get results."

* * *

Isaac Penington, 1616–1679

Penington was an early Friend and fierce defender of Quakerism, with deeply held views on its significance in terms of the lived experience of Christ. His teachings and guidance have had great impact on individuals and implications for Christian faith in the world. He wrote extensively about spiritual insight and gave solid, much-revered counsel, which seems to be caring and to carry a personal touch. His writings are tender and articulate, inspirational to this day. He was imprisoned several times for refusing to take oaths and for attending Quaker meetings.

I have had deep experience concerning the worship of God from a child, having travelled in spirit with my God for the right knowledge thereof, and in singleness of heart giving up unto him, according as he hath taught and led my poor, needy, depending soul....

An imagining

Christ is Penington's teacher, his guide, from within. His guide never leaves him and is always at his side. He gives him the strength to write, to argue, to refuse to swear and to attend meeting for worship during times when it is forbidden. Christ gives him the strength to survive harsh imprisonments and everything else that life throws at him. Penington wants us all to surrender to the guide of Christ within, so that we can give up wondering which way to go and instead follow our guide, which is there all the time.

From his writings

Heed not distressing thoughts when they rise ever so strongly in thee; fear them not, but be ***still*** *awhile, not believing in the power which thou feelest they have over thee, and it will fall on a sudden. It is good for thy spirit and greatly to thy advantage to be much and variously*

exercised by the Lord. Thou dost not know what the Lord hath already done and what he is yet doing for thee therein.
Isaac Penington (*Quaker Faith and Practice* 2.48)

Adaptation
Don't take any notice of any thoughts that upset you when they come up; don't be afraid of them, but be still for a while, and don't engage with whatever power you feel they might have over you, and they will drift away, losing their energy. It is good for you to be pushed to your limits sometimes. You cannot be aware of what has been done on your behalf already and what is still being done.

Further thoughts
Penington's words are reassuring. We can stop any of our useless "thinking" and any tendency to be swayed by powerful thoughts, but instead give our power over to being still and waiting for the advice of our guide. We are being led from that place of not knowing and not thinking. There is much that is done outside our control, without thinking and willpower being involved. What is then important is the nature of individual action in the world.

* * *

William Penn, 1644–1718

Penn was part of the second phase of Quakerism. His early life prepared him well. He came from a well-off family and was well educated, intelligent, articulate and rebellious, and this eventually led him into Quakerism, taking cues from "primitive Christianity." He traveled in ministry and was imprisoned, he wrote books and fought theological battles. Sailing to the American colonies, Penn was instrumental in setting up the model state of Pennsylvania and his caring, conciliatory relationship with the Native Americans who owned the land is what he is probably best remembered for.

An imagining

William knows Christ within. He is sure of "it" and his awareness of it has no limits. He comes from a wealthy background and has received the best schooling available. He has had every advantage and has the confidence that comes with it. He wears good-quality tailoring and his shoe buckles gleam. His collars are always crisp. He has an amiable way with him, listening carefully, with understanding. His Christianity is of the "primitive" sort and he has absolute certainty in it. This is the way for him: to live a better life is to search for the spirit of Christ that is inside us all. All we have to do is listen to the stillness and live out this message.

From his writings

Look not out, but within... Remember it is a ***still*** *voice that speaks to us in this day, and that it is not to be heard in the noises and hurries of the mind; but it is distinctly understood in a retired frame. Jesus loved and chose solitudes, often going to mountains, to gardens, and sea-sides to avoid crowds and hurries; to show his disciples it was good to be solitary and sit loose to the world.*

William Penn, 1694 (*Quaker Faith and Practice* 21.03)

Adaptation

Don't look at what is outside of you, but inside instead... Remember, it is a still voice speaking to us. You won't notice and understand it in your normal thinking self, but by resting and seeing what comes out of your inner stillness. Jesus chose to be alone often, going to the mountains, to gardens and shores to avoid bustling crowds; to demonstrate to his disciples that it was good to be alone sometimes and be more detached from the rest of life.

Further thoughts

Penn seems to hint at the spirit within and without, connecting everything. He is reminding us that we have responsibility for everything, both for our own actions and how they affect the wider community. We cannot, therefore, blame others when things go wrong but must listen instead for the still voice, communicating stillness, which is guiding us in all things.

From his writings

Love silence, even in the mind... Much speaking, as much thinking, spends; and in many thoughts, as well as words, there is sin. True ***silence*** *is the rest of the mind; and is to the spirit, what sleep is to the body, nourishment and refreshment.*

William Penn, 1699 (*Quaker Faith and Practice* 20.11)

Adaptation

Gravitate towards silence and stillness, even within yourself... If you speak too much, or think too much, or use too many words, perhaps without listening, then you might fail in your endeavors. Real, deep silence is to your mind and spirit what sleep is to your body: rest, recuperation, food and drink.

Further thoughts

Penn cautions us against too much head activity and speaking without careful reflection, or listening to ourselves rather than others: liking the sound of our own words rather than listening deeply to those of others. He advises that we might miss out on what is really important and perhaps fail in what we are trying to do. Silence can be the very thing our deepest self really needs in order to recuperate from its own restlessness and exhausting thinking, and so fulfill its own potential and do real good in the world.

* * *

Caroline Stephen, 1834–1909

Stephen, a quiet studious woman, was an encourager of others. Born into a high-flying family, sister of Leslie Stephen, who was Virginia Woolf's father, as the only Quaker in the family she has perhaps been overlooked – at least by her immediate relatives, who seem to belittle her achievements. Information about her focuses on what her male relations did in their lives and you have to dig further to find out about what she herself did. And it turns out she did a great deal. She engaged in charitable works, wrote highly acclaimed books about Quakerism, still considered classics a hundred years later.

An imagining

Caroline sits. She is quiet and careful. She is calm and still. She has a serious demeanor but inside she is positive and joyful. It is perhaps a shame that this side of her is not always apparent to others. She has an instinctive understanding of stillness. Her ministry is about caring for others and writing and educating anyone who is interested about Quakerism, especially young people. One of her young protégées is her niece, Virginia Woolf, to whom she will bequeath the money that will allow her to be independent and to write. Caroline's life has been marked by sadness, though perhaps this is more through the eyes of others than her own.

From her writings

*In the united **stillness** of a truly 'gathered' meeting there is a power known only by experience, and mysterious even when most familiar.*
Caroline E. Stephen, 1908 (*Quaker Faith and Practice* 2.39)

Adaptation

In the stillness of a truly gathered meeting, you will find a power that you will discover to be mysterious even when you become used to it through experience.

Further thoughts

Caroline comes across as a calm, thoughtful person, serious and dedicated in her various pursuits. She presents her findings as facts and suggests a direct cause and effect in relation to being in the gathered meeting.

From her writings

On one never-to-be-forgotten Sunday morning, I found myself one of a small company of silent worshippers who were content to sit down together without words, that each one might feel after and draw near to the Divine Presence, unhindered at least, if not helped, by any human utterance.... My whole soul was filled with the unutterable peace of the undisturbed opportunity for communion with God, with the sense that at last I had found a place where I might, without the faintest suspicion of insincerity, join with others in simply seeking His present. To sit down in silence could at the least pledge me to nothing; it might open to me (as it did that morning) the very gate of heaven.

Caroline E. Stephen, 1890 (*Quaker Faith and Practice* 2.02)

Adaptation

I sat in silence with others, without speaking, and we were all content in our silence, feeling that it could bring us nearer to the sacred, without any person intervening. ... I felt myself fill with the possibility of communicating with God, knowing that I had discovered a place where I could authentically seek in silence, without any obligation and perhaps open me to my own potential.

Further thoughts

Caroline stumbles upon the heart of Quaker worship in the quietness, the stillness, the lack of intervention, the community, and discovers that she responds to it and finds possibility in it. It is for her.

* * *

John Woolman, 1720–72

Woolman, in many people's minds, was the first green activist. He cared passionately about the natural world and could see how easily the early beginnings of industrialization and consumerism were already exploiting and despoiling it. Acting from a place of conscience, he saw clearly that through contemplation and inward prayer he could move out into the world, acting for good. He came from a relatively well-heeled family and could have made a very good living for himself, but he believed that capitalizing on the world was unethical and he was fervent in the mission of living prayerfully, simply and modestly, for Truth. He is well remembered for his utter rejection of the slave trade and his eccentric practice of wearing undyed clothes, aware that the manufacture of dyes was harmful and exploitative of both people and the natural world.

An imagining

Woolman acts from a place of personal Truth. He moves about, with the blessing of his meeting, convinced of the rightness of his beliefs and his actions. He is guided from within by prayerfulness and rightness that comes from silence. His confidence allows him to stand out from others and he seems a little eccentric; sometimes people are shocked. However, this does not faze him. His care for people, animals, the world – everything – is there in the way he is, for all to witness.

From his writings

The place of prayer is a precious habitation: ... I saw this habitation to be safe, to be inwardly quiet, when there was great stirrings and commotions in the world.

John Woolman, 1770 (*Quaker Faith and Practice* 20.10)

Adaptation
To be quiet in prayer is a place of great preciousness. ... I felt that going within and stilling my thoughts was a refuge when the world outside was full of disquiet and unrest.

Further thoughts
Woolman feels that his inner life can be a place he retreats to in times of stress, and finds a safe haven when life becomes too much to deal with.

* * *

What early Quaker discoveries can mean for us

Early Quakers from the seventeenth century onwards wrote extensively about how Christ was a reality in their lives and how others could access this. Among their key findings was the idea that people had no need of priests to teach individuals and act as intermediaries between themselves and God, but that they had the ability to access Christ within themselves and that there was "that of God" within all. This led to the concept that all were equal in the Quaker meeting, since no one could lay claim to being more important or more endowed with Spirit than anyone else.

Dwelling in stillness, at any time and in any place, can help us with our place in the world and ground us, forming a constant background to all our activities. Wherever we are and whatever we are doing, we can pause, go within and think "Stillness" or "Be still" or "Still." This can ground us and pull everything back into perspective. As soon as a moment of stillness has visited and percolated into the center, we can acknowledge it before returning to whatever we were doing. There will be a feeling of increased relaxation and life will seem more full and more meaningful. Once this meditation has been fully explored it can be applied to many different situations and purposes, according to whatever we need. There are examples from everyday life in the chapters that follow, but these can be adapted to suit individual needs.

- Sit comfortably and close your eyes or adopt a soft gaze.
- Pause all everyday thoughts.
- Go within to your center.
- Find the place where everything is still.
- Stay in this place until you know it fully.
- Emerge.
- Move forward with your day.

Or, taking the gist of George Fox's advice:

- 1. Be still.
- 2. Turn to God.
- 3. Receive strength.

Or from Margaret Fell:

- When you meet together, wait in **silence** upon the Lord
- That in the Spirit ye may wait.
- To worship him in Spirit.

Or, in a paraphrase of Alexander Parker's words:

- Sit down.
- Turn in to the same light.
- Wait in the spirit in pure **stillness.**
- Wait in the light.

These early Friends were all essentially imparting the same advice: sit, be still, wait, turn to the Light within, in order to find Truth. They were pointing out that we all have this ability and do not need others to tell us what Truth is. We know it in our still center.

Part II

Seekings and Findings

Meditation, in its most basic definition, is sometimes described as the act of thinking deeply and being in a state of contemplation. But it is also a method for bringing the whole self into the present moment and quieting restlessness in the mind and putting aside the head activity of "thinking." Meditation can bring with it a sense of being released from the busy mind and a bringing together of the whole of one's life into "being" rather than "doing." In the sense used in this book, it is more useful to think of meditation as a method of going within and a tool for seeking and finding stillness – leaving the "thinking" mind behind for a while, if possible. This can mean finding stillness on our own paths and examining our own lives, or it could mean branching out more broadly, into the community and the world beyond.

As Quakers, we do not always want to discuss what we do in meeting for worship, since for many this is personal, though perhaps it is true that some feel that whatever it is they "do" may not be quite "right" in some way or not quite as effective as what others may be doing. It is ironic that we have the freedom to worship in whatever way we feel works best for us, as individuals, but that sometimes we lack confidence or assume that others are "doing" it better or more effectively. Perhaps we are so used to being given instructions in our styles of education, in our work settings, and in life generally, all working towards an identified ideal, that we can't feel confident in finding our own way, knowing that it works perfectly well for us. If given the chance, however, many Quakers may be willing to articulate methods they regularly use to "go within" and still the restless everyday mind.

The meditation highlighted in this book, inspired by early Quakers' advice to sit, turn to the Light, and wait in the stillness for God can be used in almost any Quaker setting. In a meeting for worship, it may be the first thing we do when we sit down together. We still ourselves, keeping eyes open or letting them close, turning inward to that still place, and waiting. In the gathered silence of the hour, with others, there may be answers to our questions, moments of clarity, feelings of being held, helped and encouraged, personal illumination and love for others. Ideas also come to the fore and long-held struggles may seem to arrive at a point of rest. The meeting is a group activity and the "gathered" feeling is a shared experience, so the meditation already described above can be a joint activity. It is also common for people to be thinking along the same lines, although they may not be aware of this until someone is moved to speak and someone else realizes that this thought was in their own mind too.

In a business meeting for worship, held from a place of silence too, but following a set agenda, there may be a need to pause proceedings and re-focus thoughts. This can be done by asking Friends to still themselves before moving to a place of feeling that a decision has come into the group and a minute can be made and agreed that reflects this. In a meeting for clearness, when an individual brings a concern to a small group of Friends, stillness is the way in which the gatheredness of the meeting eventually enables the individual to find their own way, while being held in Spirit. The technique of moving within and waiting is used. A way forward emerges, unbidden.

Sometimes it is hard to come to a point of joint "way forward." Perhaps simple discussion cannot produce a discerned solution for an issue or a problem. Rather than just continuing to talk, often repeating thoughts, taking sides and perhaps failing to listen or contributing too much, it is good to allow time for stillness. Out of this settled contemplation a more productive discussion may then take place, leading to a discerned solution for the meeting, accepted by all as the best route. There is no need to formalize a "group meditation moment," or similar, by using set steps or mantras. Each person pauses to still their voice and thoughts before going within to see where the way ahead lies. It is a matter of setting the self aside in favor of the group.

Supporting the concerns and methods of the meeting and its processes in terms of "leadership" roles can sometimes feel like a heavy burden. Who are we to feel we are fit to take on a role of authority? We may feel nervous and ill-equipped, but gradually confidence and strength can come and we can know how to act and what to do. In the end we just have to support each other and do what needs to be done. Meditating on stillness, either singly or as a group, within, can help find the way forward. It can feel as if this is a gift that has been given to us.

The meditation can be used to make decisions about practical matters to do with the functioning of the community. This can include issues such as the care of a building, what to do about a problem, when to act and in what way, how to respond to a request in right ordering, how to care for someone who is unwell, how to "elder" someone with sensitivity and love.

In a Quaker setting, accessing stillness might be useful for:

- Deciding to nominate someone for a Quaker role.
- Deciding to accept or decline a Quaker role.
- Helping someone to make an important life decision (in a meeting for clearness).
- Deciding to terminate someone's role because of conflict.
- Deciding to encourage an attender into Quaker membership.
- Visiting someone who wants to come into Quaker membership.
- Visiting a couple intending to have a Quaker wedding.

Chapter 3

Looking Within

Kol Nidre

Kol Nidre, the night before Yom Kippur, begins the Day of Atonement for Jews. We atone for wrongdoings of the past year and ask God for forgiveness. The Kol Nidre is the prayer that marks the beginning of the service. Beforehand we meditate and reflect. One meditation is from Ecclesiastes 5:3–5.

> *When you make a promise to God, do not delay in fulfilling it, for He has no pleasure in fools. Whatever you vow fulfil. It is better not to vow than to vow and not fulfil. Let not your mouth cause guilt to your body and plead before the collector 'it was just a mistake'. Why should God be angry at your speech and destroy what you have achieved?*

The meditation period ends and the beautiful Kol Nidre begins. Every time I hear it I am connected to Jews past and present – it begins my reflection of my life and my silent discussions with God.

Ann Berne

Until you have looked within, you cannot look outward to help others or move forward in action for yourself, for the community or for the world. You cannot act from a good place of knowing. Or, at least, you can't do it effectively. So it is important to work on yourself first and create more self-understanding, self-knowledge. During meditation you may receive insights.

There are questions you could ask: Who am I? How am I? Why am I? Where am I in my life? Are there things I find difficult? Are there things I want to change, but feel unable to do so? What are they?

Perhaps some or all of these questions are not right for you. If this is the case, adapt them according to whatever you need.

Once you have searched within, you might find that the discipline of searching for stillness, and perhaps finding it, can help you self-explore, heal and then act in a way that suits you. Perhaps a good place to start is with "nothing" and build up from that place. So start with "Emptying out your center" and "Doing nothing," until it becomes obvious what you need, and clear how you might act.

What follows are examples of how the meditation can be used for looking within. The wordings of the meditations are different from the original basic version (see page 42), but the practice is essentially the same every time.

The suggestions range from fairly minor problems to far bigger ones. Tailor them to suit you and your life – your personal needs and wishes. Information and learning can be built up gradually. Each meditation example sets out the basic meditation wording and then gives a suggested way of changing the words, sometimes including visualization. Choose other wordings to suit you better, if desired, and add your own issues. If necessary, repeat the meditation later, on successive days. You may find that solutions, answers and "findings" come to you later, when you have moved on to another activity.

1. Emptying out your center

Sometimes we might be held back in our endeavors if the mind is too full of thoughts: plans and commitments, "oughts" and "shoulds." The window may need cleaning or the floor may need sweeping, but these things can wait until you have done this meditation. And there are always worries. The key is to prevent them from dominating. It may feel as though we have to clear away the whole lot first, before thinking about doing something as time-consuming and even as self-indulgent as meditating, if that's the way it feels. Sometimes it's about valuing the self and making that the priority. Try to de-clutter, even empty, yourself as a priority. Later it will feel as though meditating is as essential as taking a long drink of water or breathing in a lungful of fresh air – and utterly worthwhile.

Before you start meditating, you need to feel that your head and heart are clear of everyday thoughts that you do not need for a while. Aim to feel that there is a clear space within that you can use for a purpose – for yourself. Therefore you may need to put aside anything that is already there, which does not serve you at the moment. If you make this a conscious act, you will find more intention within yourself to make something happen – for you. The very fact that you have reserved time and space proves your intention, so you can build up from that place: from now.

The meditation

- Sit comfortably and close your eyes or adopt a soft gaze.
- Pause all everyday thoughts.
- Go within to your center.
- Find the place where everything is still.
- Stay in this place until you know it fully.
- Emerge.
- Move forward with your day.

Adaptation

- Sit comfortably, close your eyes or let your gaze unfocus.
- Locate your everyday thoughts, such as lists and commitments, which you will not need for the next few minutes, and visualize placing them in a small box. Put this on one side.
- Go to the space that has been left empty within you, now that your thoughts have been put to one side.
- Dwell on the stillness within you that now fills that empty space.
- Remain there in stillness as long as you need to. If you want a mantra to focus on, choose "Space" or a word that suggests positive emptiness to you.

- When you have spent as long as you need in stillness, emerge into the present, perhaps visualizing taking your thoughts out of their box again and looking at them with fresh eyes.
- Move ahead with your day.

2. Doing nothing

Sometimes it feels wrong to do "nothing." Surely there is something we "ought" to be doing: something useful, necessary and productive. Perhaps women, particularly, feel this to be one of their special pressures, because we are so used to doing, doing, doing and "trying to get things done." Often, this is doing things for others, if we are used to being in caring roles in life. First, perhaps what we think of as "nothing," is in fact "something." It could be that what seems to be inactivity is the pause we need before launching into further activity, with direction, intention and a result in mind. So it is far from being nothing. It is necessary. There is no need to be doing something all the time. There is time for rest, for reflection, for space, for nothingness, where something can happen. The issue to be resolved here, perhaps, is for it to feel fine to be doing nothing, for it to be completely guilt-free. Sometimes action comes from a state of "not doing," from pausing life and letting things settle rather than jumping into action straight away. This may turn out to be mistaken, or moving in the wrong direction. We may hear a great deal about boredom and there is much fear of this state. But this too is necessary. Once you have experienced this somewhat bleak place, the only way is upward, into ideas and action. Boredom can be a launch pad for effective action.

The meditation

- Sit comfortably and close your eyes or adopt a soft gaze.
- Pause all everyday thoughts.
- Go within to your center.

- Find the place where everything is still.
- Stay in this place until you know it fully.
- Emerge.
- Move forward with your day.

Adaptation

- Sit comfortably, in whatever way you prefer. Keep your eyes open.
- Settle into a state of staring into space. Or stare at something that draws your gaze: a picture, a photograph, a floor or a ceiling.
- Do not "think," just gaze, gradually directing yourself towards the stillness within you.
- Find deep-seated value in your gaze. Find meaning in it.
- If you need to add a mantra to hold your mind, try "Nothingness."
- Very soon, from a position of inner stillness, you will become aware of the importance of all your actions and appreciate them all equally.
- As you gradually surface, you will know what you need to do next.

3. Finding peace even if silence is absent

Each person needs to find their own version of inner peace, even if they feel powerless to act in the world, which may feel very troubled. Some find peace in swimming or being with trees; others find it in music or dancing and in all these things silence is far from absent: water splashes, trees rustle, music is music and dancing can be part of it. We can help each other remotely by finding a calm place in our own lives. To feel unsettled spreads fear and negativity. It is not necessary to experience silence when searching for peace, since it may be an unrealistic state and out of reach; sound is everywhere, all around us. Feeling peaceful cuts through the silence into a place of stillness and inner calm.

The meditation

- Sit comfortably and close your eyes or adopt a soft gaze.
- Pause all everyday thoughts.
- Go within to your center.
- Find the place where everything is still.
- Stay in this place until you know it fully.
- Emerge.
- Move forward with your day.

Adaptation

- Sit quietly and settle into as calm a state as is possible – for you. Keep your eyes open and softly focused, or closed if you prefer.
- Observe your breath moving naturally in and out. You might focus on hearing the breath or feeling its cool touch inside your nose.
- If fearful thoughts start to creep in, try to let them float away and return to your breaths again. Start again when you are feeling calmer.
- Move within until you find a place of stillness, of peace, and stay there for a few moments. If you want to use a mantra, try repeating "Peace."
- Emerge, and acknowledge any feelings you may have of being in a state of greater peace. This may not be apparent straight away.

4. Finding self-acceptance

You are okay just as you are. This might sound like a cliché, way too simple, but it is good to accept this fact if you find yourself constantly thinking about ways to "improve" yourself and your behavior. We are only human and there has never been, and never will be, a "perfect" person. We are all flawed – and all wonderful. This is not to feel that you have already done "enough," but to feel that you are who you are and cannot turn yourself into what you are not. You are not broken and you do not need "fixing" according to someone's else's vision, or what you think this might be. Perhaps the key to finding self-acceptance is to explore who you really are, rather than who you think you are. This meditation might be useful and play well if you are worried about the aging process, fading with the years, and find yourself dwelling on it. We all have to get old – if we are lucky enough. Perhaps the aging process is a privilege rather than an endurance.

The meditation

- Sit comfortably and close your eyes or adopt a soft gaze.
- Pause all everyday thoughts.
- Go within to your center.
- Find the place where everything is still.
- Stay in this place until you know it fully.
- Emerge.
- Move forward with your day.

Adaptation

- Sit in a comfortable place and close the eyes or let your eyes unfocus.
- First, think about "you" or however this idea presents itself to you. This may not feel comfortable at first.
- Go deep, to your center and perhaps use the mantra "Me" or "Me-ness" if that helps improve your focus on stillness. Alternatively, concentrate on the breath. In and out.
- Remain in the "Me'" place within for as long as you can, feeling the stillness as completely as you can.
- Staying with "Me" or "Me-ness," explore all that this word means for you, negative and positive. Look at the "Me" from all directions and visualize this from above, from below, from both sides – from all angles. Perhaps form an objective appreciation of this version of yourself. Visualize

moving outside yourself and see what you are looking at.
- When your thoughts start to kick in again, emerge.
- Continue with your day, perhaps feeling more in tune with the essence of "You."

5. Being content to be on your own

Is there something wrong about being by yourself and enjoying it? Stillness can be accessed in a group, but finding stillness alone allows you to really find depths in it.

According to societal "norms," the state of being alone is not something that is often sought after. Life is reflected back to us, by media, and by each other, as something that must be experienced in pairs and couples, groups and gatherings, and because this is not necessarily our present state we may feel "different" and outside what is thought of as being usual in society. We may feel "wrong." But it is fine to be on one's own – and to enjoy it.

Sometimes it seems as though everyone else you know is a happy part of a couple or a family, a group or a community – but you are not. You might want to be, but this is not to be. Rather than pining for something that is out of reach at present, be content to make the most of the situation you are in now. Enjoy your own company and make the most of solitude. Get to know yourself.

The meditation

- Sit comfortably and close your eyes or adopt a soft gaze.
- Pause all everyday thoughts.
- Go within to your center.
- Find the place where everything is still.
- Stay in this place until you know it fully.
- Emerge.
- Move forward with your day.

Adaptation

- Sit comfortably and close your eyes or maintain soft focus.
- Take a few moments to go within by watching the breath. In and out.
- Go into the stillness of your very center.
- Dwell on what this place feels like. Perhaps try the word "Alone" as a mantra and keep on repeating it.
- Stay in the "Alone" place for a while and explore its essence as deeply as you can. Go right into the feeling of solitude and remain there as long as you can.
- Find whatever it is that makes you content to be you and be with yourself – find further hints of positivity and even happiness in that zone.
- If your mind wanders off, just draw it back to "Alone" again. Visualize your thoughts as if they are a restless, curious dog on a lead that wants to keep on darting off but needs gently pulling back again.
- When you have got what you need from this time in stillness, return gradually to everyday life. Perhaps you will find more acceptance in yourself.
- As you continue with your day, resist the temptation to miss the presence of others, however hard that is.
- Carry on being with yourself and being content with that state. Repeat the meditation several times.

6. Standing aside and "holding"

Sometimes being a witness is all that is required of you in a given situation. You do not need to act and this is not what is required of you this time. Resist the temptation to get involved, if this doesn't feel right. Others may be better suited. Your role is to "hold" what is going on, in the hope and trust that things will be resolved.

In a Quaker setting, this approach can apply to rotating roles and duties. Perhaps you are called to "hold" others in the activity or the space in the Light and to facilitate whatever is happening to happen. We are active bystanders and we need to be in touch with our own stillness and the stillness of others. Perhaps it is not for us to be the one to come up with the idea to solve the problem but rather to allow others to do it and to hold the space in which this can take place. Your role may be to suggest holding quiet reflection in which stillness can work on the issue. It is important to be a presence rather than trying to influence progress and outcomes. It is vital to be humble and to hold on to equality.

The meditation

- Sit comfortably and close your eyes or adopt a soft gaze.
- Pause all everyday thoughts.
- Go within to your center.
- Find the place where everything is still.
- Stay in this place until you know it fully.
- Emerge.
- Move forward with your day.

Adaptation

- Sit in meditation, with eyes closed or softly unfocused.
- Relax and go within to your center.
- Watch your breath – in and out.
- Visualize the situation you want to witness. See it before you, in your mind's eye. Perhaps it has already happened but you want to learn from it for next time. Perhaps it is a situation that is coming up, which you want to be sure about holding rightly.
- Go deep within so that the situation seems real to you, so that you feel you are living it. If you want to use a mantra, try "Witness" or "Hold."
- Stay with it, in the stillness of your center.
- When you feel satisfied that the meditation has benefited

you, return to your day.

- When the day of the situation or event comes (if the event is in the future) – think back to this meditation and perhaps visualize reliving parts of it. Stillness will return to you.

7. Abandoning "fear of missing out"

People often complain that they feel that everything of importance and positivity is happening somewhere else and that they are not there to be part of it – they feel they are missing out and this produces anxiety and alone-ness. This is a feeling that can embed itself early in life and still be present later as a feeling of gravitating to past memories or future anticipations, but never the present. There is an unsettling mood of wanting to be there, in the center, doing what the crowd is doing and being part of it. However, this is not always possible or even desirable.

The meditation

- Sit comfortably and close your eyes or adopt a soft gaze.
- Pause all everyday thoughts.
- Go within to your center.
- Find the place where everything is still.
- Stay in this place until you know it fully.
- Emerge.
- Move forward with your day.

Adaptation

- Sit comfortably with eyes closed or softly unfocused.
- Rest as deeply as you can, breathing in and out. Watch your breath.
- Go within to access your stillness, in your center.
- If a mantra would help you center, try "Self."
- If your mind wanders off in directions of its own choosing, just let the thoughts drift off and return when you become

aware of what's happening. Repeating "Self" will help.
- Remain in this space of stillness for as long as seems right.
- When you are ready, surface from the meditation.
- Resume your activities. Hopefully you will feel more focused and self-contained, confident in your own actions. If results are unclear or unsatisfactory, repeat the meditation on successive days until you feel you don't need to any more.
- As days go by you may feel more contented in your own company.

8. Finding meaning

What is your life for? What is your purpose? You are here for a reason, but you may not yet know what it is. Or you may have hints and inklings. There is no answer to this, but it may be good to explore, even if an answer remains obscure at first. It is up to each individual to decide what their own purpose is and not for anyone else to tell them. It's a good subject to ponder from time to time, just to keep focused on doing what is really important rather than what you "think" is important or what you think others think is important. A good example of this might be that others may think that accumulating wealth and possessions is important, and you might get sucked into this mindset over time. Look at why you might feel different, and then hold that thought in a positive light. Thinking about these issues, from a place of stillness, will reveal that some things are not important to you beyond a certain point. Maybe your purpose is to keep on searching, with mind wide open.

The meditation

- Sit comfortably and close your eyes or adopt a soft gaze.
- Pause all everyday thoughts.
- Go within to your center.
- Find the place where everything is still.

- Stay in this place until you know it fully.
- Emerge.
- Move forward with your day.

Adaptation

- Sit comfortably and close your eyes or maintain a soft focus.
- Sink within yourself and relax as completely as you can.
- Focus on the breath, in and out, or adopt an appropriate mantra, which could be "Meaning," or similar. Choose something that appeals to you and seems to sum up the situation.
- Spend some time in this deep place of stillness. If your mind wanders, thoughts drifting in and out of your awareness, draw them gently back to "Meaning." Visualize your thoughts as being rather like a kite on a long string. Let them fly away, but draw them carefully back to you occasionally.
- Take as long as you like in this phase.
- When it seems right, emerge and get on with your day.
- At some point, possibly later, it may feel as though you have reached some kind of resolution of the word "Meaning" in your life. If results do not seem satisfactory, repeat the meditation as many times as you need to on successive days.

9. Dealing with difficulty

Difficulties are part of life. The moment you think you have sorted them all out, another one pops up to get your attention and perhaps make you feel anxious. The meditation approach, diving into stillness, can be applied to almost any ongoing difficulty in life. Using inner resources helps deal with fresh levels of difficulty, possibly some never encountered before. The more difficult things become, the better you become at dealing with them. You are strong and you become even stronger.

Practice makes perfect.

Meditation can come to one's assistance, even if the benefits may not seem obvious straight away. Sometimes it might feel as though nothing is happening, but then, a while later, you may find resolution and answers coming to you unexpectedly.

The meditation

- Sit comfortably and close your eyes or adopt a soft gaze.
- Pause all everyday thoughts.
- Go within to your center.
- Find the place where everything is still.
- Stay in this place until you know it fully.
- Emerge.
- Move forward with your day.

Adaptation

- Sit in a relaxed state, close your eyes or settle into soft focus.
- Go within to find your state of personal stillness, deep within your center.
- Gradually settle on any negative thoughts or problems in your mind today: personal difficulties, money worries, job concerns, family problems, fears for the future – whatever it is you are worried about.
- Choose one difficulty, in particular, to focus on.
- Sit with this one difficulty in stillness and go right into it, as deeply as you can. Try to look at it from every possible angle.
- Hold this state for as long as you can. If you feel like surfacing from it, resist that impulse and sit with it for a little while longer.
- After a time, when you sense that you have really gone as deeply as you can, rise to the surface again.
- Sit with whatever feelings come up now.

- Open your eyes and move on with your day.

10. Finding your path

The way forward is not always clear or straightforward. You may find it hard to see what you need to do next or there may be a range of options to choose from. If there is a "fork in the road" to be chosen, but your usual thought patterns do not give you a solution, try meditating on the issue as objectively as you can before making a final decision. From a place of stillness, try to look at yourself from above, as a separate being, and see what you might suggest for that other person, who is you, objectively. Perhaps you could visualize flying above yourself, like a drone, looking down on this figure who is facing an important decision.

The meditation

- Sit comfortably and close your eyes or adopt a soft gaze.
- Pause all everyday thoughts.
- Go within to your center.
- Find the place where everything is still.
- Stay in this place until you know it fully.
- Emerge.
- Move forward with your day.

Adaptation

- Sit comfortably and close your eyes or have them half-closed with soft focus.
- Try to pause your restless mind and bring it down to focusing on this issue before you. Perhaps distill the issue into one word, such as, "Which?" or "What?" and come back to this when your mind wanders.
- Visualize yourself as a figure moving along a path in a landscape. Create the scene however you would most like it to be. It could be a woodland walk, fringed with plants and flowers, trees on either side or perhaps a rocky

hilltop path.

- Move your attention to a spot above yourself, floating, and look down on yourself.
- If your mind wanders, return it gently to the word "Which?" or "What?"
- Visualize hanging above yourself, looking down, for as long as you need to, seeing the figure of yourself moving along.
- Your figure comes to a fork in the path. Focus on the words "Which?" or "What?" for as long as you can.
- See whether you feel inclined to take one path or the other. Don't force your progress. If it seems right to just stand still, do so for a while, until you feel ready to move on again.
- Return to yourself and emerge from the meditation.
- Go about your day. Later you may find that you know the answer to your decision, without even thinking about it any more. If this does not happen, repeat until you are satisfied.

Chapter 4

Healing

Childhood memory

As a small child, I was drawn to the stillness and incense-scented hush of our parish church. The church was old and large, and the thick stone walls kept out any noise, and there was very little outside noise anyway. I remember being out on a walk with the dog – I think the current one was a fox terrier named Rusty. In that time and place, a child of about seven or eight out by herself with a dog was not considered unsafe. I pushed open the heavy door, thought that although God would not mind, perhaps the dog should not run around in the church, and tucked her under my arm. The church was dim, just the sanctuary lamp burning over the altar, and very very quiet. This little vignette has stayed with me. True stillness.

Rosalind Patterson

Once you have "gone within," to a greater or lesser extent, and even if this part of the process is far from complete, you will already have started healing. You may be either healing yourself or healing others – or both. One state can lead to the other. You may not even be aware that you can heal others, but you can. Sometimes just listening to someone or even holding them in the Light may eventually lead to healing outcomes.

Here are some examples of how the meditation can be used for healing. The suggestions range from fairly trivial problems to far bigger ones. Tailor them to suit you and your life – to your personal needs and wishes. Each meditation sets out the original meditation and then gives a suggested way of changing the words. Sometimes visualization is included. Change the wording according to whatever suits you best. If you want to, repeat the meditation on successive days. You may find that outcomes arrive at a later time, when you are involved in something quite different.

1. Holding people in the Light

You can feel great pain if those close to you are going through difficulties. Perhaps you are too far away to help in a practical sense, or you may not want to let the person know you are worried about them. But you still want to do something and add your support, though perhaps without their being aware of it. You will feel empowered in doing something, even though you may feel powerless. You may find that focusing your deepest thoughts on a person in trouble could help them, even if you cannot quite say why. This could be called "prayer" or "holding in the Light," though you may not choose either of these phrases. Whatever you choose to call it, the process itself can help them – and help you too.

The meditation

- Sit comfortably and close your eyes or adopt a soft gaze.
- Pause all everyday thoughts.
- Go within to your center.
- Find the place where everything is still.
- Stay in this place until you know it fully.
- Emerge.
- Move forward with your day.

Adaptation

- If you want to hold the person in the Light using stillness, stop everything, including all your flying thoughts, and bring that person to the front of your mind.
- In your visualization, keep them there for as long as you can, in the loving stillness of your heart. Use the word "Light" as a mantra, if you want to, or you could use the person's name.

- Wish for the person whatever it is that they want or need, regardless of your own opinions or views. Bring your own energy into action through stillness.
- When your concentration falters, let the person go and continue with your day.
- Return to this process, for this person, as much as you can, whenever it occurs to you – until the difficulty is resolved.

2. Helping recovery

Getting your life back after an illness, an accident, a shock, bereavement or an unwelcome life change, can take a long time and needs much patience. You have to be a kind friend to yourself and not expect to just jump back into your life as it once was. Acknowledge that things have changed. You have changed. You have to go slowly and not expect too much all at once. Trying a regular healing meditation can help you get back on track and resume your normal life. Be prepared for the process to take time, even though part of you is desperate to feel that you are back to your old self.

The meditation

- Sit comfortably and close your eyes or adopt a soft gaze.
- Pause all everyday thoughts.
- Go within to your center.
- Find the place where everything is still.
- Stay in this place until you know it fully.
- Emerge.
- Move forward with your day.

Adaptation

- Sit comfortably in a quiet space and close your eyes.
- Turn your attention within to your center.
- Perhaps choose a word that can help your mind return to

this center whenever it wants to wander away. You could try, "Return" or "Heal."

- Dwell on the part of yourself that feels hurt or damaged and bring all your attention to it, in your still center.
- Stay in this spot for as long as you can, visualize bathing it with healing gold light.
- Let the gold light expand and grow, bathing your whole body. It might feel a bit like sunbathing.
- Rest in this gold light for as long as you can, feeling the "normal" you slowly returning to life.
- When you have stayed in the place for long enough, return to your everyday state.
- Do this meditation every day, in the same way, and start to feel that you are healing as well as you are able.

3. Tackling negativity

Negative feelings and thoughts flowing into your mind can destroy natural positivity and start dragging you down, but you can use stillness to help such feelings float away. A first step might be to own negative thoughts, realizing that they are our responsibility and that we have the power and ability to transform them into positivity. There is a realization that there is no point in blaming anyone or anything else. If you wake up feeling positive, only to be assailed by creeping negativity later on, try this technique early in the day. Later remember that moving about, drinking water, eating a snack or taking a nap may give immediate assistance, since inactivity, hunger, thirst or tiredness may be part of your negative mood. Physical pain may be affecting your mood too.

The meditation

- Sit comfortably and close your eyes or adopt a soft gaze.
- Pause all everyday thoughts.
- Go within to your center.

- Find the place where everything is still.
- Stay in this place until you know it fully.
- Emerge.
- Move forward with your day.

Adaptation

- The moment you realize you are lapsing into negative thinking, resolve to do something about it straight away rather than sinking further.
- Sit comfortably and close your eyes. Or maintain a soft gaze.
- Take a few moments to access stillness within.
- Using the energy of your stillness, shift your attention in the direction of positive plans. Make a mental list, which could be mundane. Think, "First I will do this and then I will do that." This will put you back in control of finding the positive. Or you could turn your attention to fulfilling appealing personal plans and projects. Hold these things close, one at a time, for a short time, in the stillness.
- When you are ready, come back to the day and resume your activities.
- Decide what you will do first. Then do it. The mere act of making a start on something will help you to feel better.
- Move on to the next thing. Little by little you will find yourself in a more positive place and the negativity will drift away.

4. Listening more effectively

The world is full of noise and the desire and ability to express oneself is now thought to be more important than the ability to listen, really listen, to others. The individual is thought to be more important than the group. This has led to high levels of self-centeredness. Some people seem to have a lot to offload but are not really interested in hearing what others have to say.

There is no exchange and they are involved in themselves and their own lives. This state may be temporary, but their selves fill up their thoughts and exclude all else. However, if people are heard, properly, they do start to heal. If someone needs you to listen to them, hear them and be with them in their deepest hurts in that moment. Sit back, relax, and from your place of inner stillness, transmit stillness to them. If you find it hard to remember what anyone has said or anything about people you have spoken with, perhaps try the meditation to allow you to take interest in others – genuine interest.

Try meditating (alone) in order to prepare yourself to listen fully and completely.

The meditation

- Sit comfortably and close your eyes or adopt a soft gaze.
- Pause all everyday thoughts.
- Go within to your center.
- Find the place where everything is still.
- Stay in this place until you know it fully.
- Emerge.
- Move forward with your day.

Adaptation

- Do this meditation on your own. Just hold the other person in your mind.
- Sit in comfort with eyes closed or adopt a soft gaze.
- Breathe in and out, relaxing your whole body. Resolve to put your own ego, and what you think and might want to say, into the background for the moment.
- In visualization, make steady eye contact with the person, but without being invasive, intrusive or threatening.
- Visualize the person starting to speak. Let them go on without feeling the need to interrupt or answer. Pay your fullest possible attention. If a response seems called for,

just think "yes" or "mmm."
- When the person has stopped talking, think along the lines of, "That must be hard for you."
- If you think about speaking, do so from a position of recalling everything the person has told you, because you have given them your entire attention.
- When you have explored this situation fully, resume your day. The next time you meet the person, you may find that things have improved.

5. Dealing with feeling drained

This is not about not getting enough sleep (see page 63), but rather being weighed down by the pressure of having too much to achieve; too many demands. This may well be self-imposed, so perhaps first look at why this might be. Or it could be about feeling that the confidence has seeped out of you and your wellbeing is disappearing. Sometimes your list of things that need to be done (see page 76) can be long and it seems vital to "get them done" before you can stop worrying and relax. Things prey on the mind, adding to the feeling of being constantly exhausted. It is as though there is an ever-present pressure, with no chance of resting. Some things need attention – for example, there may be an emergency. This feeling can be very debilitating and lead to being "dragged down." It can take over life. Perhaps dealing with this comes low on the list of priorities. However, other things can be left until you have more time and energy – often combined with the right kind of mood. Meditating on stillness may come to your assistance.

The meditation

- Sit comfortably and close your eyes or adopt a soft gaze.
- Pause all everyday thoughts.
- Go within to your center.
- Find the place where everything is still.

- Stay in this place until you know it fully.
- Emerge.
- Move forward with your day.

Adaptation

- Sit in a comfortable space and close your eyes or gaze softly.
- Pause all everyday thoughts and visualize parceling up the things that worry you, leaving them on one side.
- Go within to your center and perhaps focus on the mantra "Relax."
- Keep returning to this mantra whenever your mind wants to drift off. It is like a child who wants to keep moving.
- Remain in your still place of relaxation until you feel you know it fully and have explored it as far as you can.
- Surface from your meditation.
- Move forward with your day, perhaps feeling more relaxed and with more energy to do one thing at a time, with satisfaction.

6. Helping sleep

There is plenty already written about how to improve sleep patterns, but meditation really can help to relax and calm you, so it is worth trying to find stillness during sleepless times. If you are wakeful and struggle to drop off, even lying still while watching the breath can take you to a different place, away from the worry about not sleeping. It can prepare you for drifting off again. The act of focusing on the breath alone will calm the mind and prevent it being flooded by thoughts and worries. If thoughts really do invade, perhaps thinking about very mundane daily things rather than the bigger issues will calm you too.

The meditation

- Sit comfortably and close your eyes or adopt a soft gaze.
- Pause all everyday thoughts.
- Go within to your center.
- Find the place where everything is still.
- Stay in this place until you know it fully.
- Emerge.
- Move forward with your day.

Adaptation

- When you find yourself awake when you don't want to be, try not to fret.
- Lie still comfortably with eyes closed. Don't turn on lights or use electronic devices. Just stay still and quiet – otherwise your mind will start to get active. If your mind has already starting whirring, still it by drawing it towards a mantra such as, "Stillness" or "Quietness."
- Turn to the breath and focus your attention on it: in and out. Either hear it passing in and out or feel the cool of it passing through your nostrils.
- Whenever your mind starts to wake up and get active, bring it gently back to the mantra or the breath. Do this repeatedly if you need to.
- Stay in your place of quiet stillness and savor the silence of the night.
- Keep returning to it.
- Before long, you will wake to a new morning, feeling refreshed and anticipating the day.
- If the meditation does not seem to be improving things at first, repeat it on successive days.

7. Finding stillness in visual things

So often we are only looking at our own thoughts and our eyes are turned inwards. Searching for meaning in all you see may feel too open-ended, but really looking, seeing and finding joy in what lies before your eyes can ground you. Don't search for what seems visually "appealing" – just take meaning from what is already before you, wherever you are. Perhaps look at the levels of blueness stretching towards a distant horizon or mesmerizing wave patterns, the shapes made by intersecting blades of grass, or a pile of pebbles. If nature is not available to you, look at the way a shadow affects the objects in the room, or the way colors change during the day.

The meditation

- Sit comfortably and close your eyes or adopt a soft gaze.
- Pause all everyday thoughts.
- Go within to your center.
- Find the place where everything is still.
- Stay in this place until you know it fully.
- Emerge.
- Move forward with your day.

Adaptation

- Keeping eyes open, let your gaze rest upon something outside of yourself: a shadow, a pleasing arrangement of shapes, a seductive pattern, contrasting colors that appeal to you – and let them sink into you.
- Absorb them into yourself, making them a part of you. Let the stillness of what is outside you go within.
- Repeatedly draw your wandering mind back to what you are gazing at. Find new things in it that you did not notice before. There may be new layers, depths or textures.
- Gradually your mind will still in your center.
- Remain in this place for as long as you need to.
- When you feel ready, come to the surface again and resume your day.
- Later, you will be able to recall exactly what your eyes

absorbed and thereby the moment of stillness you were given.

8. Making decisions

Sometimes being decisive is a problem. We may feel caught between what we ought to do and what we should do, what our duty-self is telling us is the "right" thing, and what feels right for our souls. We feel torn in different directions. Sometimes both aspects feel right; at other times neither. First one, then the other. The mind bounces back and forth, finding nooks and crannies to rest in for a while, before taking off and veering in the other direction, which now feels like the right one. Taking a pause and diving into meditation to find stillness may provide an answer, not immediately, but in the end, with patience.

The meditation

- Sit comfortably and close your eyes or adopt a soft gaze.
- Pause all everyday thoughts.
- Go within to your center.
- Find the place where everything is still.
- Stay in this place until you know it fully.
- Emerge.
- Move forward with your day.

Adaptation

- Sit comfortably with eyes closed or open, using soft focus.
- Go within, perhaps using a mantra such as, "Answering."
- If your mind flies away, like a bird, wheeling away on a breeze, only to circle around and coming to land away from you, focus on the mantra.
- Rest in this still place for as long as you can – until it feels fully explored.
- Come back to the surface, to your thoughts, to your conundrums, and resume normal life.

- Some time later, a decision may become obvious to you. Just when you weren't expecting it.

9. Finding balance in life

Life may give us a feeling of walking a tightrope. Balance is often hard-won and difficult to maintain. A split-second of loss of concentration and we could fall down on one side, or the other. We have different things to pursue and keep going all at once, and this sometimes feels tough – if not impossible. Things conflict with each other. However, it is important to keep all aspects of life flourishing at once, otherwise we can become one-sided creatures – overly focused on one aspect of our skills and talents, obligations and duties, which then grows out of all proportion, becoming larger and larger, like an over-used muscle. Sometimes it might seem as though when you are active in one part of your life, you are pining after another, which you are missing. And vice versa. Satisfaction in life may be hard to find. Bringing the mind into the present moment can help. Perhaps you can find fulfillment and enjoyment in whatever you are doing, now.

The meditation

- Sit comfortably and close your eyes or adopt a soft gaze.
- Pause all everyday thoughts.
- Go within to your center.
- Find the place where everything is still.
- Stay in this place until you know it fully.
- Emerge.
- Move forward with your day.

Adaptation

- Sit, relax in your quiet place.
- Go within, with eyes closed, to the still place within.
- Perhaps choose a mantra to help you focus. This might

be, "Balance." Whenever your mind wants to take off and explore, bring it gently back to this word.

- Remain in the stillness of your center for a while.
- When you are ready, return to normal life.
- Soon you will find that you are balancing well on the tightrope that is your life, without having to think about it.

Chapter 5

Action

Stillness
Silence quickening, slowly deepening
Awareness growing, presence, stillness
My body softens, settles in quietude
People come and go in awareness
Words enter the stillness, rising falling
We meet each other in the mystery
I am part of, yet separate
Conscious being amongst conscious beings
I rest in being.
Judith Wilkings

What does "action" mean and what can *you* do? How can you look outside yourself? Action can mean small things or big things, or perhaps there is a move from one to the other. There may be aspects of life that you want to change. Now is the time to use your skills to act in the world. Action can be empowering, allowing you to take back your skills, your usefulness and your positivity for your life and for others.

Here are some examples of how the meditation can be used for action. As before, the wordings of each meditation vary from the original basic version, but the practice is essentially the same.

The suggestions range from fairly trivial problems to far bigger ones. Tailor them to suit you and your life – your personal needs and wishes. Each one sets out basic meditation and then gives a suggested way of changing the words. Sometimes visualization is included. Choose a form of words that suits you best. Be aware that you may need to repeat the meditation on successive days and that you might not notice any changes or insights until much later, when you have had a chance to move on to a different activity. Results may come, but they are always unbidden.

1. Giving up addictive activities

You might want to give up something small or something big. An addictive habit might be something you have slid into gradually, but which you now need to abandon. It is not serving you. This could be the way you think about someone and the way you relate to them, which is damaging for both of you, or not useful to either of you. Or it could be one of the issues that may spring to mind in terms of "addiction": drinking, eating, gambling, shopping – there are many, it could even be that you are addicted to a person. Whatever it is, and whatever its scale, accessing your stillness can help you make a start and move towards challenging and changing habits. Remember that beginnings may be small, but small things can lead to bigger things.

The meditation

- Sit comfortably and close your eyes or adopt a soft gaze.
- Pause all everyday thoughts.
- Go within to your center.
- Find the place where everything is still.
- Stay in this place until you know it fully.
- Emerge.
- Move forward with your day.

Adaptation

- Sit comfortably and close your eyes or let your eyes relax into a soft gaze.
- Go within, holding the thing you feel addicted to in your center, so that it fills it, becoming your whole center.
- If it helps, adopt it as your mantra: "Drink," "Clothes," "Cake."

- Keep returning to your mantra for as long as possible. Whenever your mind veers away, draw it gently back, like a dog on a lead. Perhaps your mind does not want to acknowledge it.
- Stay with the mantra for longer than seems possible – and then go on for a little bit longer.
- After a while of being in this place of stillness, surface and return to your normal life.
- See if meditating in this way makes a difference. If it does not, keep on repeating the meditation every day. Results may come later, when you are least expecting it.

2. Finding something that is lost

Use inner stillness to solve practical problems, even quite mundane ones. You may have mislaid something. The fear of losing something important will not leave you, it is so irritating, so you start thinking obsessively about the last time you had it, where you might have put it – all the possible places. You cannot think about anything else. You blame yourself. You try to visualize where it might be. Do not be tempted to pull everything out in a panic. Perhaps try doing something else or letting a night's sleep go by without continuing your search, either physically or mentally. You may like to try visualizing the "thing" that you have lost as a box tied up with colorful ribbon, a gift, which may come to you at a later time. You may feel you have lost something more intangible: your way in life, perhaps? If so, use the same meditation but visualize a winding road or a path.

The meditation

- Sit comfortably and close your eyes or adopt a soft gaze.
- Pause all everyday thoughts.
- Go within to your center.
- Find the place where everything is still.

- Stay in this place until you know it fully.
- Emerge.
- Move forward with your day.

Adaptation

- Sit comfortably and close your eyes or adopt soft focus with eyes open.
- Go within and let feelings of urgency and self-punishment drift away. They will not help you.
- Find your stillness, within and without.
- If it helps, choose a mantra to help your focus. This needs to be a positive word that you like, such as, "Find," "Again," "Near."
- Remain in your stillness for a while and if your mind wants to explore, gently pull it back towards your mantra again. Visualize your mind as being a balloon on a ribbon, tied to your wrist.
- When you have gone as far as you can, emerge from this state and continue with your day. Focus on other concerns.
- Later you may suddenly be able to pinpoint where the lost object is and find it again, seemingly effortlessly. This moment of enlightenment will come unbidden. If it does not, repeat the meditation as many times as necessary and then move on to other activities. The missing item will pop into your mind unbidden and you will be able to go straight to it. If you are trying to find your way in life, an idea or a solution might suddenly come up when you are least expecting it.

3. Getting a perspective on possessions

Many books and articles have been written on this subject, but perhaps stillness can contribute to the discussion. We own too many things and they may all seem important. The act of purchasing may seem irresistible. There may be deep-seated reasons for this. We have a tendency to gather in and keep more, and more, and this can interrupt feelings of stillness in life. There are many reasons for wanting to gather, own and hang on to possessions, but if you need to change this state, perhaps accessing stillness in meditation can help. Whether it is weeding out things, with a view to downsizing, creating space for other activities, or suddenly recognizing that someone else might be able to use what you do not need, perhaps now is the time to let go of some things. In the first instance, be kind to yourself. Perhaps you could just keep the things that really mean a lot to you and dispose of the rest. Bear in mind that the need to de-clutter could apply to activities or people in your life, too.

- Pass on things you no longer use or value to someone who may like them more than you do.
- Get rid of things that are leftovers from times when you were less happy or which remind you of less-happy times.
- Remember that things are just things; they cannot give you love and they may fill your living space with their burdensome negativity and deadness, which is dragging you down, holding you back.
- Keep things that seem to be "lucky" or talismanic in some way. They are charged with good energy that will bring solace and stillness.
- Keep things that were talismanic for those dear to you, but which are now in your possession.

When you have collected together a pile of items that you might want to let go of, take each one in turn and contemplate it using the meditation:

The meditation

- Sit comfortably and close your eyes or adopt a soft gaze.
- Pause all everyday thoughts.

- Go within to your center.
- Find the place where everything is still.
- Stay in this place until you know it fully.
- Emerge.
- Move forward with your day.

Adaptation

- Hold the item that you might let go of and close your eyes or let your eyes rest with soft focus.
- Go within to the place of stillness and hold the item in the center of your attention.
- If it helps your focus, choose a mantra to draw your mind back whenever it wants to wander away. Helpful words might include, "Release," "Fly" or "Soar."
- Rest in this place for as long as you need to. Draw your mind back to the mantra when it wanders, which it certainly will.
- Emerge from the stillness and place the item you are considering in a special place, on its own.
- Carry on with your day.
- The next time your eyes rest on the item, perhaps it will be clearer whether you still need to keep it or not. If answers do not emerge straight away, repeat the meditation. Or you can place the item on one side and review the issue a few days later. An answer will come.

4. Putting your phone in its place

On a long train journey, through the dark, a woman was talking on her phone whilst tapping on her laptop. She was explaining how she was going on a week-long retreat in a remote place, in which there would be complete silence. There would be no electronic devices allowed, no screen-time and no communication. There were mixed feelings about eavesdropping, but this couldn't be helped. Thoughts arose about how it was going to be for her and potentially how life-changing. Technology is designed to be addictive, insidiously so, to make it hard for people to resist. They become addicted to it, losing something very important in the process. What do they lose? Perhaps time, specifically "empty" time.

This exercise addresses the "phone," but it may apply to other devices too. Adapt it to your own needs.

Perhaps this is a good time to think about what the phone represents. It seems to exert great power – so much so that people feel unable to ignore it and bereft if they have to. The phone seems to dominate many situations. People give way to its perceived importance. It absorbs time and creativity, but it is also a useful tool when it doesn't rule. If you think you are looking at your phone too much and would rather be doing other things, this exercise is about reassessing possible addiction to it and regaining perspective and control over your life. This approach can be applied to other habits you may want to alter too.

The meditation

- Sit comfortably and close your eyes or adopt a soft gaze.
- Pause all everyday thoughts.
- Go within to your center.
- Find the place where everything is still.
- Stay in this place until you know it fully.
- Emerge.
- Move forward with your day.

Adaptation

- Using soft eyes, gaze at your phone on the table in front of you.
- In a state of inner stillness, think about it and nothing else.
- Think about your feelings for this object and the emotions

it may arouse: love, hate, anxiety? Or a mixture of these?
- Dwell on what this item means for you and your life. How does it make you feel?
- How would you feel if you lost it? Go to the center of any feelings of panic and stay there for as long as you can, exploring deeply.
- Now mentally put your device on one side or on a shelf and re-center. Stay in this place for as long as feels useful.
- When you are ready, come back to the present moment and think about how you feel towards your device now. Is there any shift of attitude? You may feel more detached from it. You may not notice change immediately.

Variation
- Use your device all day, from the moment you wake up until the moment you fall asleep, including eating and drinking, talking to people, walking about. Avoid lampposts if you can. Use it for as many different purposes as you can (finding things out, finding your way around, shopping and planning, entertainment, music, communicating, explaining yourself, expounding your views, displaying things you have done/eaten/visited, photographing and videoing, tracking finances, spending and saving). Keep the phone in your hand at all times. Take it to the bathroom with you.
- Explore your feelings and moods in relation to your phone.
- Consider whether you felt still at any point during your day.

5. Tackling your to-do list

Perhaps you have too many things on your to-do list and they are all fighting for attention. If your thoughts are troubled and you do not seem able to calm them down, but you have a lot to do, try focusing on the short-term issues first of all and make a resolve to deal with the bigger ones later – when your storm has passed over and your clouds have cleared. Isolate just one thing, which is perhaps more urgent or just easier to accomplish, and get that one thing done. Resolve to leave the rest for a better time and open your mind to different things – perhaps more relaxing or enjoyable things.

The meditation

- Sit comfortably and close your eyes or adopt a soft gaze.
- Pause all everyday thoughts.
- Go within to your center.
- Find the place where everything is still.
- Stay in this place until you know it fully.
- Emerge.
- Move forward with your day.

Adaptation

- Firstly, spend time thinking, "Just for today I'm going to do one thing only."
- Then sit comfortably and close your eyes or gaze softly.
- Go within to a still place.
- Meditate on the mantra, "One thing", for a while.
- Stay with this as long as you can, in a place of stillness.
- When you are ready, emerge from the place of stillness and start carrying out the "One thing."
- When that is done, relax and refrain from thinking about the rest of the list until tomorrow. Repeat this meditation whenever this issue needs revisiting.

6. Stopping procrastinating

Many of us postpone difficult tasks until the deadline is almost on top of us, or we are in the "right" kind of mood. It can be done "later," but it is there lurking at the back of the mind, ever-present. If only we could just do it and then it would be out of the way, gone – until next time. Perhaps we even feel that we "need" the pressure of a deadline to motivate us in the first place. This kind of thinking, which may go all the way back to completing school homework, can play havoc with our lives, even though we may find ways of justifying it, believing that we perform best under pressure and so on. Meanwhile the task, which may be quite straightforward really, grows out of all proportion, into a looming giant. It threatens our peace of mind. Like a tongue exploring a tooth cavity, the mind returns again and again to the painful place of the task not being done – yet. Stillness can help with this.

The meditation

- Sit comfortably and close your eyes or adopt a soft gaze.
- Pause all everyday thoughts.
- Go within to your center.
- Find the place where everything is still.
- Stay in this place until you know it fully.
- Emerge.
- Move forward with your day.

Adaptation

- Sit comfortably and close your eyes or gaze softly.
- Pause all thoughts of the task that you have been avoiding or putting off for a better, more suitable, time.
- Go within to your still center and see if there is a mantra that can help you stay there. Choose a word that appeals to you, such as "Light."
- Whenever your mind wants to fly away, return to "Light" again and again.
- Stay in this place of "Light" until you know it fully.
- Emerge from the depths, like bubbles breaking the surface.
- Move forward with your day, which may, or may not,

involve getting on with the task you have been avoiding.

- Make a plan for completing the task and you will find that you stick to it. Repeat the meditation if it doesn't seem to be touching the spot. The effect may come unexpectedly, much later on.

7. Maintaining attention – a reminder

The meditation is all about focusing your attention, but we end here with a reminder of its value. It needs to be revisited and maintained. Gradually, with practice, it becomes easier to go within and find stillness, *your* stillness, and this, in turn, improves skills for focusing and concentrating on anything at all. It becomes a habit that can lead to great feelings of positivity. You are bringing awareness to the need to focus and this is already setting you on the right path to better concentration, better thinking, calmer living. Just being aware that your thoughts are likely to float away, right when you want them to be present, is putting you in the way of improving your ability to maintain attention. Then you can go further in your actions and be more effective in the world.

The meditation

- Sit comfortably and close your eyes or adopt a soft gaze.
- Pause all everyday thoughts.
- Go within to your center.
- Find the place where everything is still.
- Stay in this place until you know it fully.
- Emerge.
- Move forward with your day.

Adaptation

- Sit comfortably and close your eyes or gaze softly, unfocused.
- Be present for yourself, in this time, in this place.

- Go within to your center of stillness. If you wish to use a mantra to assist you, and draw your mind back whenever it drifts away, choose "Focus" or a similar word that appeals to you. Whatever works for you is the one to go for.
- Find the place within yourself where everything is full of stillness.
- Stay in this place until you know it fully. If your mind wants to go off and find something more interesting to attach itself to, become aware of this, without irritation, discomfort or annoyance, and gently draw it back.
- After a while, when you feel you have explored this place fully, gradually rise to the surface again.
- Move forward with your day – in light and love.

Epilogue

Stillness is always there – at any time, in any place – at your core. You always carry your stillness with you. Meditation can offer you a helping hand to access its power.

* * *

Give over thine own willing; give over thine own running; give over thine own desiring to know or to be any thing, and sink down to the seed which God sows in the heart, and let that grow in thee, and be in thee, and breathe in thee, and act in thee, and thou shalt find by sweet experience that the Lord knows that, and loves and owns that, and will lead it to the inheritance of life, which is his portion.
Isaac Penington, *Some Directions of the Panting Soul,* vol. 2, 1661

* * *

Becoming a seal: Finding self-acceptance
Striving for this and that
No definite goal, a need to prove myself
Why? To whom?

Oh to be rid of the niggling guilt
So,

I step out of the house
Away from the road
Onto the shore
Shed the clothes
Move towards the waves, foamy edge
Into the smooth, silky chill
Deep breaths in and out

In and out in time with the waves
Become one with the sea, numbing cold
Numbness becomes freedom from fear
Unseen creatures
Alarming tickling from wafts of seaweed

I dive under
And down
Speeding with the current
Flicking flippers propel me back up
To the light.

Sally Wright

About the author

Joanna Godfrey Wood has been a Quaker all her life and attended Quaker school. She recently took the Equipping for Ministry course at the Woodbrooke Quaker Study Centre in Birmingham, England. This gave her a chance to study many aspects of Christianity and Quakerism, in the course of which she studied the works of seventeenth-century Quaker Margaret Fell, particularly her writings about the Light. She also looked at the connection between creativity and ministry in a more general way. In her local Quaker meeting she is an elder and her particular ministry is facilitating study groups for local Friends. Joanna spent her working life as a book editor, of both fiction and non-fiction titles. She has also written *Travelling in the Light: How Margaret Fell's writings can speak to Quakers today*, published by The Kindlers, 2019, and *In STEP with Testimony: Simplicity, Truth, Equality and Peace – inspired by Margaret Fell's writings*, Christian Alternative Books, John Hunt Publishing Ltd, 2021.

Bibliography

Ambler, Rex, *Truth of the Heart: An Anthology of George Fox*, Quaker Books, 2001

Bittle, William G., *James Nayler 1618–1660: The Quaker indicted by Parliament*, Friends United Press, 1986

Kagge, Erling, *Silence in the Age of Noise*, Penguin Random House UK, 2017

Godfrey Wood, Joanna, *Travelling in the Light: How Margaret Fell's Writings can Speak to Quakers Today*, The Kindlers, 2019

Godfrey Wood, Joanna, *In STEP with Quaker Testimony: Simplicity, Truth, Equality and Peace – Inspired by Margaret Fell's Writings*, Christian Alternative Books, John Hunt Publishing, 2021

Hawkins, David R., *Letting Go: The Pathway to Surrender*, Hay House UK, 2014

Holiday, Ryan, *Stillness is the Key*, Profile Books, 2019

Kabat-Zinn, Jon, *Full Catastrophe Living*, Little Brown, 2013

Kabat-Zinn, Jon, *Coming to our Senses*, Hachette, 2005

Lewis, Hunter, *The Essence of George Fox's Journal*, Axios Press, 2012

Maitland, Sara, *A Book of Silence*, Granta Books, 2009

Odell, Jenny, *How to do Nothing: Resisting the Attention Economy*, Melville House Publishing, 2019

Quaker Faith and Practice, The book of Christian discipline of the Yearly Meeting of the Religious Society of Friends (Quakers) in Britain, 1995

Peck, M. Scott, *The Road Less Travelled*, Arrow, 1990 (new ed.)

Peck, M. Scott, *The Road Less Travelled and Beyond*, Rider, 1997

Post Abbott, Margery, *Walk Humbly, Serve Boldly*, Inner Light Books, 2018

Punshon, John, *Portrait in Grey: A short history of the Quakers*, Quaker Home Service, 1984

Also in this series

Quaker Roots and Branches
John Lampen

Quaker Roots and Branches explores what Quakers call their 'testimonies' – the interaction of inspiration, faith and action to bring change in the world. It looks at Quaker concerns around the sustainability of the planet, peace and war, punishment, and music and the arts in the past and today. It stresses the continuity of their witness over three hundred and sixty-five years as well as their openness to change and development.

Telling the Truth about God
Rhiannon Grant

Telling the truth about God without excluding anyone is a challenge to the Quaker community. Drawing on the author's academic research into Quaker uses of religious language and her teaching to Quaker and academic groups, Rhiannon Grant aims to make accessible some key theological and philosophical insights. She explains that Quakers might sound vague but are actually making clear and creative theological claims.

What Do Quakers Believe?
Geoffrey Durham

Geoffrey Durham answers the crucial question 'What do Quakers believe?' clearly, straightforwardly and without jargon. In the process he introduces a unique religious group whose impact and influence in the world is far greater than their numbers suggest. *What Do Quakers Believe?* is a friendly, direct and accessible toe-in-the-water book for readers who have often wondered who these Quakers are, but have never quite found out.

THE NEW OPEN SPACES

Throughout the two thousand years of Christian tradition there have been, and still are, groups and individuals that exist in the margins and upon the edge of faith. But in Christianity's contrapuntal history it has often been these outcasts and pioneers that have forged contemporary orthodoxy out of former radicalism as belief evolves to engage with and encompass the ever-changing social and scientific realities. Real faith lies not in the comfortable certainties of the Orthodox, but somewhere in a half-glimpsed hinterland on the dirt track to Emmaus, where the Death of God meets the Resurrection, where the supernatural Christ meets the historical Jesus, and where the revolution liberates both the oppressed and the oppressors.

Welcome to Christian Alternative... a space at the edge where the light shines through.

If you have enjoyed this book, why not tell other readers by posting a review on your preferred book site.

Recent bestsellers from Christian Alternative are:

Bread Not Stones

The Autobiography of An Eventful Life

Una Kroll

The spiritual autobiography of a truly remarkable woman and a history of the struggle for ordination in the Church of England.

Paperback: 978-1-78279-804-0 ebook: 978-1-78279-805-7

The Quaker Way

A Rediscovery

Rex Ambler

Although fairly well known, Quakerism is not well understood. The purpose of this book is to explain how Quakerism works as a spiritual practice.

Paperback: 978-1-78099-657-8 ebook: 978-1-78099-658-5

Blue Sky God

The Evolution of Science and Christianity

Don MacGregor

Quantum consciousness, morphic fields and blue-sky thinking about God and Jesus the Christ.

Paperback: 978-1-84694-937-1 ebook: 978-1-84694-938-8

Celtic Wheel of the Year

Tess Ward

An original and inspiring selection of prayers combining Christian and Celtic Pagan traditions, and interweaving their calendars into a single pattern of prayer for every morning and night of the year.

Paperback: 978-1-90504-795-6

Christian Atheist

Belonging without Believing

Brian Mountford

Christian Atheists don't believe in God but miss him: especially the transcendent beauty of his music, language, ethics, and community.

Paperback: 978-1-84694-439-0 ebook: 978-1-84694-929-6

Compassion Or Apocalypse?

A Comprehensible Guide to the Thoughts of René Girard

James Warren

How René Girard changes the way we think about God and the Bible, and its relevance for our apocalypse-threatened world.

Paperback: 978-1-78279-073-0 ebook: 978-1-78279-072-3

Diary Of A Gay Priest

The Tightrope Walker

Rev. Dr. Malcolm Johnson

Full of anecdotes and amusing stories, but the Church is still a dangerous place for a gay priest.

Paperback: 978-1-78279-002-0 ebook: 978-1-78099-999-9

Do You Need God?

Exploring Different Paths to Spirituality Even For Atheists

Rory J.Q. Barnes

An unbiased guide to the building blocks of spiritual belief.

Paperback: 978-1-78279-380-9 ebook: 978-1-78279-379-3

Readers of ebooks can buy or view any of these bestsellers by clicking on the live link in the title. Most titles are published in paperback and as an ebook. Paperbacks are available in traditional bookshops. Both print and ebook formats are available online.

Find more titles and sign up to our readers' newsletter at
http://www.johnhuntpublishing.com/christianity
Follow us on Facebook at
https://www.facebook.com/ChristianAlternative